I0074605

Teen Entrepreneur's Roadmap

10 Steps to Success Before Graduation

James J. Mintwise

© Copyright 2024 - All rights reserved.

The content contained within this book may not be reproduced, duplicated or transmitted without direct written permission from the author or the publisher.

Under no circumstances will any blame or legal responsibility be held against the publisher, or author, for any damages, reparation, or monetary loss due to the information contained within this book, either directly or indirectly.

Legal Notice:

This book is copyright protected. It is only for personal use. You cannot amend, distribute, sell, use, quote or paraphrase any part, or the content within this book, without the consent of the author or publisher.

Disclaimer Notice:

Please note the information contained within this document is for educational and entertainment purposes only. All effort has been executed to present accurate, up to date, reliable, complete information. No warranties of any kind are declared or implied. Readers acknowledge that the author is not engaged in the rendering of legal, financial, medical or professional advice. The content within this book has been derived from various sources. Please consult a licensed professional before attempting any techniques outlined in this book.

By reading this document, the reader agrees that under no circumstances is the author responsible for any losses, direct or indirect, that are incurred as a result of the use of the information contained within this document, including, but not limited to, errors, omissions, or inaccuracies.

Table of Contents

Introduction

Let's kick things off with something cool to think about. Did you know that by reading, you're joining a special group of people? They're called visionaries or explorers. So, if you desire to learn and improve, know that you're in good company with others who love to grow!

But here's the thing: Just wanting something isn't enough to help you get it. It'll take more than just *desire* and excitement, for instance, to finish reading all the chapters in this book. For its part, *Teen Entrepreneur's Roadmap* is exciting all the way through, but you need something extra to keep going strong. That something is called grit. Explore these questions to understand how determined you are to achieve success.

Do you really want to be a successful entrepreneur?

Think about why you want to be an entrepreneur. Is it because you're passionate about solving problems or creating something new? Or maybe you want to make a difference in your community or even the world?

Are you committed to finishing everything you start?

Reflect on your past projects. Have you seen them through to the end, even when they got tough? Being an entrepreneur means sticking with your ideas and plans, no matter the obstacles.

Are you ready to face the challenges that stand between you and your goals?

How have you handled difficulties in the past? Are you willing to learn from failures and keep pushing forward?

If you said no to those questions or felt unsure, don't worry. They're tough if you take them seriously. The solution is to imagine what you want to be recognized for. Close your eyes and think about the best version of yourself as an entrepreneur. What do you see yourself selling? It doesn't have to be something everyone knows about. It just has to make you feel excited! In many cases, determination tends to be a product of excitement and obsession. So, what really gets you going? Once you have your answer, you can go back to the questions.

If you answered the questions positively, this means you're ready.

So, let's get you set for the adventure ahead. To become an entrepreneur, you'll need to follow these seven steps.

- Think up a cool business idea.

- Create something awesome.

- Test your idea.

- Plan your business.

- Get the money you need.

- Show off your business.

- Keep growing.

In this book, you'll discover how to tackle each important step of your journey and stand out in the business world. Don't stress if you're not a business expert; and remember, age doesn't hold you back. Need proof? Look at Cory Nieves.

When Cory was just six years old, he started an amazing adventure that motivated many to follow their dreams and pursue what they love.

It all began with a simple desire to help his mother buy a car. Cory's entrepreneurial spark ignited in Englewood, New Jersey, where he started selling hot cocoa. However, his ambitions didn't stop there. With unwavering determination and a heart full of dreams, he expanded his offerings to include lemonade and, eventually, cookies. Together with his mother, Cory started baking and creating original recipes that captured the hearts and taste buds of many. His vision and dedication caught the attention of notable companies like Aetna, Barney's, Bloomingdale's, Citibank, J. Crew, Macy's, Mercedes-Benz, Pottery Barn, Ralph Lauren, TOMS, Viacom, Whole Foods, and Williams-Sonoma. Through strategic partnerships, Cory expanded his brand's reach and cemented his place as a rising star in the business world.

Then, there's Kenan. Born on March 5, 2004, in the vibrant city of San Diego, his journey toward entrepreneurship and community service began at a young age.

From his earliest days, Kenan was instilled with a spirit of compassion and a drive to help others. Raised by parents who emigrated from Turkey to the United States in pursuit of a better life, Kenan learned the value of empathy and hard work from his family. At the tender age of 11, Kenan founded Kids4Community, a nonprofit organization dedicated to combating homelessness and raising awareness among teenagers in San Diego. Through Kids4Community, Kenan and his team work tirelessly to provide meals for the homeless while educating young people about the challenges faced by those less fortunate.

Here we see the powerful story of an entrepreneur who's inspired by his desire to help people, instead of the usual motivator: money. This isn't to say that you shouldn't have profit as your primary goal. That's totally fine. If there's anything to take from this story, it's the fact that every businessperson is entitled to their own priorities. So, what inspires you?

One of Kenan's most significant achievements came in 2016 when he spearheaded a food drive that collected over 6000 cereal boxes for local shelters. His dogged commitment to making a difference earned him widespread recognition, including the prestigious title of national honoree in the 2017 Prudential Spirit of Community

Awards. Despite his busy schedule as a young entrepreneur and philanthropist, Kenan also excels in athletics. A talented triathlete, he proudly represents the San Diego area on the Men's Cross Country team at Yale University. So, if you've struggled with the question of how you could run a successful business *and* have a life, know that it is possible! It all comes down to your priorities and how you structure each day of your life. We'll see a clearer picture of how to balance work and life later in this book.

These are just two testimonies in a sprawling sea of success stories! If you ever start to doubt yourself, just remember Cory, Kenan, and others like them who have succeeded despite the clear odds stacked against them.

With that said, the exciting first chapter of this book is waiting for you. Turn the page (or scroll down) and seize your destiny!

Chapter 1:

Discovering Your Passion

If you ask someone about their passions, chances are they'll give you a rundown of fun things they enjoy. But this isn't the kind of passion through which profitable million-dollar businesses are born. A lot goes unsaid when the topic of passion is discussed. In this chapter, we'll talk about passion in its fullness and see why it is necessary for entrepreneurial success.

Historical Significance of Passion

Passion has shaped and reshaped the world in quite dramatic ways, and as a young person with dreams of becoming an entrepreneur, what you know about its historical significance can inspire and guide you. If you turn the pages of history, you'll see the powerful force that is passion driving individuals to achieve extraordinary feats, and it can do the same for you.

Innovators, leaders, and visionaries (your group, remember?) were often driven by a deep desire to make a difference. Their passion helped them overcome obstacles and push boundaries. Consider Thomas Edison, whose passion for invention led him to develop the electric light bulb despite numerous failures. He famously said, "I didn't fail, I just found 10,000 ways not to make a light bulb." Come on, that's a crazy level of passion and dedication. Or Marie Curie, whose passion for science drove her to make groundbreaking discoveries in radioactivity, even in the face of significant challenges.

When balanced with careful planning and self-awareness, it's almost magical the heights to which passion can take you!

The origin of the word "passion" itself reveals another important truth worth discussing. Derived from the Latin word *passio*, which means "suffering," passion is often linked to enduring hardship for something meaningful. This might sound scary because no one wants to suffer. Well, no one except the entrepreneur who believes that no amount of pain is too high a price to pay for the glory they seek. This willingness and almost illogical determination to face challenges and setbacks is a common trait among successful entrepreneurs.

Your passion for your business idea will consistently reenergize you, even when the path toward realizing your dreams seems unattainable to everyone around you. Whether it's developing a new product, crafting a marketing strategy, or building a brand, your passion will infuse your work with energy and something that seems all too rare today: authenticity.

Passion to Entrepreneurs

The analysis of the relationship between passion and entrepreneurial pursuit, like the one you're set to undertake, is inexhaustible. The more we study this force (passion), the more amazing knowledge we run into.

One of the coolest things about passion is that it makes you stand out. Ever tried to engage someone who genuinely loves what they do in a conversation about their interests? A few minutes into the discourse and you might feel pulled by the magnetism of their excitement! Now, you might think this has to do with their personality, but it's more likely the case that they've been entirely possessed by passion.

And you too can have the same effect on others. You could be pitching your business idea, selling your product, or just talking about your plans. But if you're sold on your dreams (if you're passionate), people will be drawn to your energy. This can pull in customers, partners, and even investors who want to share in your excitement and eventual greatness.

But what happens when things don't go as planned? Every entrepreneur has bad days. Even the most experienced business-person can miscalculate and get burned by the market. However, the passionate business-person never sees setbacks as reasons to quit. Instead of quitting; in the tradition of Edison described earlier, they become creative.

You might agree that when you care deeply about something, you're more likely to think outside the box. This creativity is often ramped up in the darkest moments of business pursuits. However, the leader of such a business should have—you guessed it, passion! This trait also helps entrepreneurs be more persistent in refining their ideas and bringing them to life, even if it takes multiple tries to get it right. It's in the flames of setbacks and passion-fueled creativity that they establish strong core values for their business.

What are core values, you ask? It's really simple. They're the guiding principles that shape who we are and how we act. Values like honesty, kindness, and respect influence our behavior and choices and encourage other people to act positively toward us. As such, the values that will form the foundation of your company culture shouldn't just be buzzwords you found while Googling "core values." There should be a richness and depth to them. This sense of purpose can be incredibly motivating, both for you and for those who work with you.

Dark Side of Entrepreneurial Passion

As we've seen, entrepreneurial passion often energizes individuals to create and grow their ventures, but this intense dedication isn't always great. There are instances where fiery passion negatively impacts the personal well-being and business performance of entrepreneurs.

Heard about burnout?

Entrepreneurs often become so consumed by their work and their desire to win that they neglect rest and personal time. They work excessively long hours in their pursuit of success. Sadly, this (in extreme cases) is destructive to the physical and emotional well-being of the entrepreneur. Their health and productivity are burned to a crisp, and we might observe this in their diminished decision-making abilities, stifled creativity, and ineffective leadership.

The deep emotional investment in their business, coupled with high stakes, weighs heavily on passionate entrepreneurs. This constant worry can lead to chronic stress, which has severe implications for mental health, including the big bad duo: anxiety and depression. For some entrepreneurs, their work overshadows other important aspects of life. Family, friends, and having some fun with life is necessary to reach the very attainable goals of happiness and contentment. When they're neglected, the individual may feel sad, lonely, and lost.

In many cases, the business suffers with the entrepreneur. This is especially the case if they play an active role in the venture. Passionate entrepreneurs may become overly controlling or demanding, expecting their team to match their level of dedication. Employees are unlikely to succeed in such intense environments. This then leads to frequent turnover (this is when employees leave companies) which disrupts business operations and damages company culture.

Entrepreneurs who are intoxicated by their vision can sometimes be blinded to market realities. They might miscalculate at the worst possible times, for instance, overestimating customer demand or underestimating costs. Ultimately, what results is a domino effect of financial challenges and business failure.

Entrepreneurs have to beware that their identity isn't so deeply entwined with their business, as it might be too difficult to disengage, even temporarily. You want to be passionate, but not addicted. You want zeal and control.

Case Studies

The Kumarans

Shravan and Sanjay Kumaran, the brilliant brother duo from Chennai, India, are making waves as the nation's youngest entrepreneurs. Back in 2011, when Shravan was 12 and Sanjay just 10, they launched their own tech company, GoDimensions. This was no ordinary childhood venture; their dad, Kumaran Surendran, had kindled their love for programming early on, and the boys quickly mastered it.

By the time they officially started GoDimensions, they had already developed over 150 test apps. Their first major hit was the app Catch Me Cop. They went on to create a bunch of cool apps, including Alphabet Board and Colour Palette for education, and Emergency Booth and Superhero for creativity. These apps have now reached users in over 50 countries.

The Kumaran brothers quickly made it into the "30 Under 30" list and were recognized as the youngest mobile application programmers by Apple. This recognition was just the beginning. They pursued computer science degrees at Texas A&M University, continuing to build on their impressive skills and knowledge (Sharma, n.d.).

Hart Main

Hart Main was the typical 13-year-old, making jokes about his sister's "girly" scented candles. This playful jab turned into an atypical lightbulb moment: Why not create candles with scents that appeal to guys? Thus, the idea for ManCans was born.

The concept was simple but brilliant: develop candles with masculine scents like campfire, bacon, fresh-cut grass, sawdust, and even "Santa's beard." These weren't your average candles. To give them a twist, Hart decided to package them in recycled soup cans, adding a rugged, upcycled charm to the products.

With ManCans, Hart really wanted to have a positive impact on the community. From the start, he had charity as an important aspect of his business model. For every candle sold, a portion of the proceeds was donated to local soup kitchens. This socially conscious decision made customers feel good about their purchase—who does want to spend money and be happy doing so? It also set ManCans apart from other candle companies who weren't as rooted in giving back.

The impact of Hart's idea was enormous. Over time, ManCans managed to donate over 100,000 cans of soup to those in need and contributed $35,000 to food-related charities. As ManCans grew, so did Hart. He learned valuable lessons about business and responsibility. Even though managing a business while balancing schoolwork and a social life wasn't easy, Hart found a balance and made it work.

Passion is super important for success, and it's as unique as your fingerprints. Seriously, no two passions are the same! Sometimes people try to take on someone else's passion, but that usually doesn't work out. You've got to find your own passion, and there are some cool ways to figure it out (Williams, 2011).

Exercises to Identify Your Passions

Brainstorming

Brainstorming is a common way to stimulate creativity, generate a plethora of ideas, and pinpoint *your* passion. Brainstorming is beloved for its simplicity. That is, if you do it correctly.

The Brainstorming Process

Here's a guide to get you started:

- Set the stage: Find a comfortable space where you can relax and think without distractions. You should also have a notebook or a digital device ready to jot down your ideas.

- Define your goal: Clearly state the purpose of your brainstorming session. For this exercise, your goal is to identify your passions. Write this at the top of your page: "What am I passionate about?"

- Free thinking session: Allow yourself to think freely and write down every idea that comes to mind. This is not the time to filter or judge your thoughts. Open the gates and let your imagination run freely.

- Encourage variety: Think about different areas of your life: hobbies, subjects at school, types of activities, and even dreams you've had—including the ones you get when you go to sleep. The more diverse your ideas, the better.

Coming Up With Many Ideas

At this stage, always keep in mind that quantity is more important than quality. The primary purpose of brainstorming is to think up and write down numerous ideas. If you run out of ink in your pen and need to get another, that's awesome! It's also cool to document your ideas digitally. Here are some prompts to help get the juices flowing:

- Interests and hobbies: What activities do you enjoy in your free time? List everything, from reading and playing sports to drawing or playing video games.

- School subjects: Which subjects do you look forward to? Why do they interest you? Is it the content, the way it's taught, or something else?

- Dreams and aspirations: What are your biggest dreams? Don't hold back, even if they seem impossible.

- People you admire: Who are your role models, and what do you admire about them?

If you still haven't gotten your answer, you can sharpen your questions and probe even deeper to find your passion. Ask yourself:

1. Which industries would I like to explore further? This could be technology, healthcare, education, or the arts (or any not mentioned here). You want to know what sparks your curiosity.

2. What type of work environment or company culture do I (or would I) thrive in? Do you prefer a fast-paced, dynamic environment, or do you flourish in a more laid-back, collaborative setting?

3. What would an ideal work-life balance mean to me? Consider how much time you want to dedicate to work versus other activities.

4. What values are most important to me in my personal life? Is it honesty, kindness, adventure, learning, or a mix of these values? We're getting closer to the core of who you are now.

5. What experiences or memories have brought me the greatest happiness? What were you doing, and why did it make you so happy?

6. What activities or pursuits make me lose track of time? Identify the activities that make you so engrossed that you forget about the clock.

These questions, combined with brainstorming, should reveal a few truths to you. Next, it's time to transform your passion(s) from letters on a page to form and color!

Vision Boards

You could wake up each day confused about who you are and what you should be doing, or you could be greeted by a beautiful, colorful reminder of all your dreams and passions. If you prefer the latter, then you need a vision board, stat!

To create one, start by gathering your supplies: magazines, scissors, and the likes. Look through the magazines and cut out pictures and words that catch your eye. Maybe it's a picture of a happy family, a quote that just rings true, or an image of someone doing something you dream of doing. Can't find many things you like? Then add your own artwork! Draw or paint anything that represents your goals.

Have you done that?

Now, let's make it even more personal. Remember the questions you asked during the brainstorming session? Cut out images and words that relate to those dreams. Add quotes and affirmations that inspire you. These could be sayings like "Believe in yourself" or "Dream big." This dream wall will be a visual representation of everything you aspire to be. And don't be afraid to go bold. It's your wall, after all. Use large images and vibrant colors to make your vision board pop. You might prefer a more new school method, in which case you can use digital vision board apps like Canva and Desygner. These applications make it even easier to combine images and words into beautiful and inspiring vision boards.

Here's a tip to make your vision board intentional. Place the most important goals and dreams in the center and surround them with supporting images and words. Every day, take a moment to visualize your goals and imagine them coming true. Let it remind you of your purpose, values, and passions. Whenever you feel down or unmotivated, look at your vision board and remember why you're working towards these goals.

Evaluating the Market Potential of Passion

You might feel like your passion is as precious as gold, but the market might not agree. By "the market," we're talking about your potential customers and how much profit you could make. As an entrepreneur, it's important to always see your business and its offerings from the market's perspective. And the way to do that? Research, research, research!

Start by looking at the market around your interests. Are there already successful businesses doing what you love? That's a good sign! It means there's demand. But don't stop there—look for trends, gaps, and opportunities. Maybe you love making eco-friendly fashion accessories. Research what consumers are saying about sustainable products. What are they missing? What do they love? This will help you find your unique angle.

You also want to know your target audience. This is super important. Who would be interested in your product or service? Are they teenagers, young adults, or maybe busy parents? What are their likes, dislikes, and biggest frustrations? For example, if you're into video editing, find out what features TikTok creators wish they had in their editing tools.

Next, you need to know who you're up against. Look for existing competitors in your chosen field and study what they offer.

Observe their strengths and where they fall short. Read customer reviews to see what people are raving about or complaining about. This information is gold! It will help you see where you can do better and stand out from the crowd. Are you following so far?

Okay, now for some math—but don't worry, it's simple. Market potential is all about figuring out how big your opportunity is. Here's a basic formula to help you out:

Market Size X Unit Price = Market Potential

Let's break it down with an example. Suppose you're planning to sell cool gadgets for TikTok users. If there are around 84.9 million TikTok users in the U.S. and you price your gadget at $10 each, your market potential would be $849,000,000. That's a whopping potential! Of course, you won't capture the entire market, but it gives you a good idea of the opportunity size.

Checklist

Now that you've done your research, understood your audience, scoped out the competition, and calculated the market potential, you're in a great position to make your passion profitable. Let's wrap things up with a quick rundown of everything you need to know to identify your passion and make it work.

1. Brainstorm ideas

- Clearly define what you want to achieve.

- Write down every thought that comes to you.

- Don't judge or filter your ideas.

- Explore different aspects of your life—hobbies, school interests, dreams, etc.—

21

- Ask yourself deep questions related to your fields of interest, values, and so on.

2. Check the market:

- Research online for trends and needs.

- Look for products or services similar to your ideas.

- Learn about your competitors.

- Investigate your target audience.

The business world changes fast, so you need to keep up to stay competitive. Reading this book is a great move because it's packed with valuable tips and practical advice. But remember, it's just one step on your journey. Real success comes from a commitment to continuous learning, trying new things, personal development, and, of course, passion. Once you have a clear understanding of where your passion lies, you can begin the real work of creating your business and defining the value of your offerings. In the next chapter, we'll go into detail about how to convert your passion and ideas into something more real: an actual business!

Recommended Reads

The Happiness of Pursuit by Chris Guillebeau.

- Chris Guillebeau believes that life is like one big quest. In this exciting book, he shares stories from his own incredible globetrotting to every country on Earth! Guillebeau encourages you to discover your own quests. He says that these adventures will bring meaning and joy to your life.

The Passion Test by Janet and Chris Attwood.

- In this life-changing book, the authors spill the beans on how to find your top five passions.

To download and reprint all the graphics from this book, visit: https://www.megarhino.com/teen-entrepreneurs-roadmap.

Checklist

1. Brainstorm Ideas:

- [ ] Create a mind map of things you're passionate about.
- [ ] List hobbies, interests, and dreams that energize you.

2. Research the Market:

- [ ] Explore online trends and identify current needs or gaps.
- [ ] Search for existing products or services similar to your ideas to see what's out there.

3. Narrow Down Your Favorites:

- [ ] Highlight or circle the top three ideas that excite you the most and feel achievable.

4. Gather Feedback:

- [ ] Share your top ideas with friends, family, or mentors.
- [ ] Ask for honest feedback- what do they like, and where do they see potential?

5. Assess Your Skills:

- [ ] Make a list of your strengths and talents that relate to each idea.
- [ ] Identify any new skills you need to learn to bring your idea to life.

6. Select Your Best Idea:

- [ ] Choose the idea that aligns with both your passions and strengths.
- [ ] Make sure it's something you feel motivated to pursue long-term.

7. Define Your Goals:

- [ ] Set specific goals for your chosen idea, breaking them down into short-term and long-term objectives.
- [ ] Ensure your goals are measurable and achievable.

8. Create a Step-by-Step Plan:

- [ ] Develop a roadmap with actionable steps to make your idea a reality.
- [ ] Break each step into smaller, manageable tasks to stay organized and on track.

Chapter 2:

Turning Your Idea Into a Business

So, you've found your passion, and you've got a killer idea for a business. That's awesome! But before you jump headfirst into the wild sea of business, think about the quality of the offering you're presenting to the market. Whether you're selling a service or an actual item, you need an audience to buy into it, or your idea may never take off. This means you need to take a second and, perhaps, third and fourth look (as many as you need) at your offering to make sure you're giving people not only what they want, but also a solution.

In this chapter, we'll discuss the various steps required to refine your business idea and really make it shine.

Clarify Your Business Concept

First things first; you need to get super clear about the kind of business you want to run. For instance, how would you describe your idea to a friend who knows nothing about it? Chances are that you're not a pioneer in the niche you've chosen. So, what makes your idea special?

Here are additional questions to help you nail down your concept (try to describe each one in a sentence or two):

- What is your business?

- What specific products or services will you offer?

- Who is your target audience?

Here's a go-to template for you: I help [target demographic] get [preferred outcome] by [unique solution], unlike [competitor] who [differentiating factor]. For example, if you're starting a custom sneaker business, you could say, "I help sneaker enthusiasts stand out by designing unique, personalized sneakers, unlike other brands that offer generic, mass-produced styles."

Identify the Problem or Need

At the start of this chapter, we mentioned giving customers a solution as one characteristic of a refined idea. This is because every successful business solves a problem. So, what needs are you meeting with your business? Or what need does it fulfill? The answer to these questions will reveal why people would want to buy from you.

Using our custom sneaker example, the problem might be, "There aren't enough unique and affordable options for teens who want to stand out with their footwear."

Develop Your Unique Selling Proposition (USP)

Your USP, put simply, is what singles out your business as something special. It's the special scent that pulls people away from other businesses and carries them to you (much like a cartoon character gliding toward food). To arrive at a compelling USP, ask yourself:

- What makes my product or service unique?

- How do I add value for my customers?

- Why should customers choose me over my competitors?

Staying on our example of a custom sneaker business, a strong USP could be, "We sell high-quality, hand-painted sneakers that are completely customizable, so you can wear your personality on your feet without breaking the bank."

Finding Your Tribe

You're scrolling through Instagram reels, and you stop at a video of someone reminiscing about the things they did as kids (playing with the light switch or making whirlpools in a bucket of water, for instance). You check the comments and, to no one's surprise, it's filled with people who can relate—many of them wondering about the specialness of their actions. This shows that, both in our experiences and the ways we react to them, the human race is very much (although not entirely) alike.

Your peers, for instance, are going through similar experiences and facing the same challenges as you. They, too, are learning on the job (the job being living). Connecting with peers means you have a group of people who understand exactly what you're going through. They can offer support, feedback, and sometimes, a different perspective that can be incredibly valuable. While there are people who seem to thrive in solitude, the vast majority of us are able to achieve our best selves by being part of a group.

If you're ready to be part of a tribe, you can start by joining online communities related to your interests or expertise. Attend meetups, workshops, and seminars where you can meet other young entrepreneurs. Share your ideas, listen to theirs, and don't be afraid to ask questions. The more you engage, the more you'll learn. We'll go into more depth on this subject when we discuss networking, mentorship, and building a support group in Chapter 6 of this book.

Making the Most of Your Connections

Once you've found your team, you must remember to nurture these relationships. Here are some tips to help you:

- Be respectful of their time: Come prepared to meetings, ask thoughtful questions, and show appreciation for their help. But most important of all, be on time. No one, especially today, likes to wait. Your punctuality to meetings with members of your group also shows that you've made the relationship a priority.

- Be open and honest: Share your challenges and successes openly. The more honest you are, the more valuable feedback you'll receive.

- Give back: If all you do is take, take, take, it's only a matter of time before people become less charitable toward you. Help and support others in your network. And it doesn't have to be a big thing. It could be as simple as sharing an article, giving feedback on their idea, or introducing them to someone in your network.

Creating a Unique Value Proposition (UVP)

A UVP is a clear statement that tells your customers why your product or service is different from the rest and why they should choose it. It's your chance to shine and show off what makes your idea unique and worth your customers' time and money (Byer, 2024).

To create a killer UVP, start by identifying the unique benefits of your product or service. Ask:

- What problems does my product solve?

- What makes my product or service different from what's already out there?

- How will it make my customers' lives better?

For our custom sneaker idea, you could highlight the fact that it also uses advanced orthopedic technology to achieve superior comfort and support, along with other perks like allowing customers to design their own unique patterns. The unique benefits here are clear: personalized style expression and exceptional foot health features.

Once you've identified your unique benefits, it's time to articulate them in a way that's easy to understand. You don't need fancy words or complex sentences. Keep it simple and down to earth. People love stories, especially when they can see themselves in them. Use real-life examples and case studies to demonstrate how your product or service solves problems. Maybe share a story about how someone rocked your custom sneakers at a music festival and stood out from the crowd, getting compliments all day long while their feet stayed comfortable.

Another tip is to leverage your youth. Being young is a superpower. Seriously! As a teenager, you have a fresh perspective and a natural ability to connect with your peers. Use this to your advantage. Create products or services that other young people can vibe with. Remember, your friends and classmates influence purchasing decisions too, so make something that appeals to them.

Once you have your UVP, go ahead and share it with the world. A UVP is basically what makes your product awesome and why it's perfect for your customers. It shows how your product solves their problems or improves their lives, and why they should pick yours over anyone else's. You can think of the UVP as the whole package that makes your product irresistible, while the USP is more about the specific features that make it stand out. See? Simple as UVP or USP.

The Basics of Business Modeling

What Is the Freemium Model?

The term "freemium", as you might have guessed, is a mash-up of "free" and "premium." Here's how it works: Companies offer the most basic version of their product or service at no cost. You can use it, enjoy it, and get a feel for what they have to offer without spending a dime. But, if you want more advanced features, better capabilities, or special add-ons, that's where the premium part comes in. You'll need to pay for those.

Companies aren't just being generous by giving away free stuff. There's a strategy behind it. Here are a few reasons why the freemium model works so well:

- Wider audience: By giving something for free, companies attract a lot of users who might be curious but not ready to pay upfront. This helps them build a large user base quickly.

- User experience: Free users get to try out the product and see if they like it. If they do, they're more likely to become paying customers later on.

- Word of mouth: Happy users often spread the word to their friends and family. More users mean more potential paying customers.

- Data collection: Companies can learn a lot from their free users. They can see which features are the most popular and which ones are need improvement. This feedback is super valuable.

Examples of Freemium Success

Some companies that have nailed the freemium model include:

- Spotify: This music streaming service lets you listen to music for free with ads. If you want an ad-free experience, offline listening, and better sound quality, you can upgrade to Spotify Premium.

- Dropbox: Dropbox gives you a certain amount of free cloud storage. If you need more space or advanced features like collaboration tools, you'll have to open your wallet.

- Candy Crush Saga: This addictive mobile game lets you play for free. However, if you run out of lives or want special boosters, you can make in-app purchases.

Now, although the freemium model works great for many companies, you can't just apply it to your business model without proper evaluation. Ever heard the saying, "One man's treasure is another man's trash"? It usually goes the other way around, but the point's the same: What proved valuable to one business may cause yours to struggle. The freemium model works best for digital products and services where the cost of adding new users is low. If your business has high production costs, giving away something for free might not be sustainable.

Online Creator Model

The internet has grown from a wild jungle dominated by fail videos to become a playground for creativity with a host of platforms where teens can monetize their passions. Unexpectedly, we now exist in the age of the "online creator." But what does it mean to bear this title?

Simply, an online creator is someone who produces content on the internet. YouTube, TikTok, X, Facebook, Twitch, and Instagram stars all belong in this category. Happily, there are no gates or fences preventing you from joining the fold. If you're passionate about something—whether it's gaming, fashion, music, or even science experiments—there's a place for you online.

That said, you might also be thinking about how much money you can make as a creator. While passion alone is a solid reason to start any venture, you'll need money (and lots of it) to keep the dream alive. Here are some pretty common ways to earn money as an online creator:

- Monetize your content: YouTube and TikTok, for instance, allow creators to monetize their videos. This means they show ads before, during, or after your videos, and you get paid based on the number of views and clicks those ads receive.

- Join an ad network: If you have a blog or website, you can join ad networks like Google AdSense. These networks place ads on your site, and you earn money whenever someone views or clicks on them.

- Sponsorships: Brands are constantly looking for ways to reach new audiences, and who better to help them than the creators those audiences love?

- Ambassadorships: Sometimes, brands will forge a deeper relationship with creators and make them ambassadors. These creator-representatives will regularly feature the brand in their content, attend events, and maybe even get exclusive behind-the-scenes access.

- Affiliate marketing: You promote a product or service. In turn, the brand settles you for every sale brought in through your link. Sounds like a win-win.

- Merch: Selling your own merchandise is a powerful way to make money while building your personal brand.

- Services: Providing services is a great way to make money and use your skills. You could start a gig mowing lawns, babysitting, managing social media for businesses, or even customizing sneakers. These services can help you earn cash locally or reach a bigger audience online, depending on what you're into and how you market yourself.

- Products: Making and selling products is another great option. You could bake delicious cookies, design cool bowties, or put together care packages for homeless kids. Sell your creations online on platforms like Etsy or at local events and markets. It's a fun way to connect with people and make a difference while earning some money.

The Power of a Business Plan

Plans are stressful and intimidating, aren't they? In fact, the very idea of a plan probably makes you want to give up on the business altogether. But hold on for a minute. Sometimes, all you need to do is reposition your perspective and your heart will be filled with courage and zeal once again. For business plans, you can imagine them as the concrete version of your abstract dreams.

When you have dreams about all your business could be, what comes to your mind? Can you see the strategies that take you from mere ideation to profitability? Can you see your employees? The big difference between your dreams and having a plan is research, and that should be a breeze if you're still passionate about your idea.

In this section, we'll see why business plans are essential for anyone looking to become an entrepreneur.

Provides a Clear Strategy

A business plan lays out the steps you need to take, the resources you'll need, and the timeline for achieving your goals. This clarity can help you avoid unnecessary detours and stay focused on what's important.

When you outline your strategy, you detail your business idea, target market, competition, and how you plan to stand out. This helps you understand your business better. It also prepares you for the challenges ahead. It's sort of a cheat sheet for the great test required to be a founder.

Helps in Securing Funding

You've certainly heard it said that money makes the world go round. Nowhere else is this truer than in business. Entrepreneurs need money all the time. They need it to start their businesses and keep it running competitively. Oftentimes, the money they require comes from investors, and these people aren't playing around. They want to know that your business idea is viable and that you're serious about it. So, if you want their money, be prepared to demonstrate your commitment by presenting a detailed business plan.

Helps Entrepreneurs Set Goals

Without goals, you have no clear direction and no way to measure your progress. This is a fact you may have experienced, even as a student. You've got to have a business plan to set strategic goals and be able to outline the actions needed to achieve them. It's also true that having clear goals keeps you motivated and focused, even with potholes and heavy traffic on your way to success.

Risk Management

Becoming an entrepreneur is a job for those who're tough and dogged. This is because every business comes with its share of risks. From market fluctuations to operational hiccups, there are countless factors that can throw you off course. With a business plan, you get to be a more effective Nostradamus: You get to predict and plan for potential risks.

Tracks Progress

It's always important to study your business, both in moments of failure and success. Say you tried a strategy, and it fell flat—well, why did that happen? And when your strategy outperforms your predictions, you should track that too. Having a business plan affords you a straightforward way to do this. It allows you to compare your actual performance against your projections and adjust your strategy or replicate them as needed.

Having a business plan is super important for any entrepreneur because it can help you figure out all the details of your venture. When you create a business plan, you're forced to discover and analyze every aspect of your business. This process helps you understand your objectives, strategies, and any challenges you might face. It also makes it easier to have a discussion about your business. A well-thought-out plan shows that you've considered everything. It gives you a clear way to explain your business concept, market opportunities, and strategies. This makes your discussions more convincing and shows that you're serious and committed to your idea.

A business plan is also quite useful when you're trying to get financial support, like loans or investments. If you show your detailed plan to your parents, potential investors, or banks, it can boost their confidence in your venture. It shows you've done your homework and are ready to handle the challenges of starting and running a business. Putting in the effort to write down several pages of planning info proves your dedication and seriousness, which means others will be more likely to back you up.

Components of a Business Plan

Now that you know why you need a business plan, let's piece it apart and see its various components.

Executive Summary

The executive summary is where you give a quick overview of your business. Here, you highlight what your business is about, what you're selling, who your customers are, and why your business will be successful. If your business plan were a book, the executive summary would be the introductory chapter. For instance, if you're starting a custom sneaker business, you might say, "I help sneaker enthusiasts stand out by designing unique, personalized sneakers, unlike other brands that offer generic, mass-produced styles." This is why people are encouraged to write it after they've penned the other sections.

Business Description

Your business description is your chance to explain your vision and goals. Talk about what kind of business you're starting, explain your mission (what you aim to achieve) and your vision (where you see your business in the future). For example, "Our custom sneaker business aims to revolutionize the footwear industry by offering one-of-a-kind, personalized sneakers that reflect each customer's unique style and personality. Our mission is to empower individuals to express themselves through their footwear, and our vision is to become the leading brand in custom sneakers, known for innovation and creativity."

Market Analysis

You'll have to do some research before completing this section of your plan. You want to know the current state of the industry and if there are any cool trends you should be aware of. It's also important to know your main competitors and what they are doing right (or wrong). For example, "The custom sneaker market is growing rapidly, driven by trends in personalization and unique fashion. Major competitors include established brands that offer limited customization options. However, they often lack the flexibility and individuality that we provide. Our in-depth market analysis shows a significant demand for truly personalized footwear that stands out from mass-produced alternatives."

Organization and Management

Here, you'll outline how your business is structured. This includes who's who in your company and what roles they play. If you're starting a business with friends, detail who's in charge of certain duties. For example, "In our custom sneaker business, I'm the CEO and creative director, overseeing the design and production of our sneakers. My co-founder handles the financial aspects, ensuring our budget is managed effectively. We've also enlisted a marketing expert to drive our branding and social media presence. In addition, we have a board of advisors with experience in the fashion industry to guide our strategic decisions."

Service or Product Line

Now it's time to describe your products or services. Knowing that your offerings are the whole point of the business, you want to be extra meticulous when writing about what they are, how they're made, and why they're awesome. For example, "Our custom sneaker line includes a range of styles, from casual wear to high-performance athletic shoes, each designed with the customer's personal touch. Using high-quality materials and advanced manufacturing techniques, we create durable and stylish sneakers. We also plan to expand our product line to include eco-friendly options and collaborations with artists to offer limited-edition designs."

Marketing and Sales Strategy

Without a marketing and sales strategy, your business may very well live out its entire life in your imagination. You need to know—and tell your team and investors via a business plan—various ways to attract and keep customers. For example, "Our marketing strategy for our custom sneaker business includes leveraging social media platforms like Instagram and TikTok to showcase our unique designs and engage with our audience. We will also use influencer partnerships to reach a broader audience. Our sales strategy involves an online store with a user-friendly design tool, as well as pop-up shops in major cities to allow customers to experience our products firsthand."

Funding Request

At this point in your business plan, you've demonstrated that you're an expert in your specific idea. If you need money to get your dream off the ground, the funding request section is where you should make it known. For example, "To launch our custom sneaker business, we are seeking $500,000 in funding. This will be allocated to purchasing high-quality materials, setting up our manufacturing facility, creating a robust online platform, and executing our marketing strategy. Specifically, $200,000 will go towards equipment and materials, $150,000 for the online platform and design tools, and $150,000 for marketing and initial operating expenses."

Financial Projections

This section is an extension of the funding request, except here you're talking about your future financial needs, say, over the next five years. This should include forecasts for income, expenses, and profits. Investors want to know that you have a plan for growth and that their money will be put to good use. As such, make sure your projections are based on the market research you conducted for your plan. If you can, include charts and graphs to make this section more visual and easier to understand. For example, "Over the next five years, we project steady growth in our custom sneaker business, with revenue increasing from $500,000 in the first year to $2 million by the fifth year. Our expenses will include materials, manufacturing, marketing, and operations. We expect to achieve profitability by the end of the second year."

Filling Out a Simple Business Model Canvas (BMC)

If you still can't decide on the right model for your business, you might find the Business Model Canvas (BMC) quite helpful. It's a fantastic tool for anyone looking to describe, design, or challenge their business model. It's essentially a one-page blueprint of your business that includes nine essential elements. To fill out each section of the BMC, follow these steps:

- **Customer segments**: These are individuals or businesses you aim to serve. Think about who will benefit from your product or service. Are they teenagers who love gaming, busy parents looking for quick meal solutions, or maybe businesses needing efficient software solutions?

- **Value propositions**: This is where you highlight the unique value that makes your product or service superior to all others in the market. What makes you stand out from the crowd? For instance, if your business delivers

39

food, your value proposition might be the speed of delivery and the convenience it offers to busy people. Think about it this way: if you were your customer, what would make you come back?

- **Channels:** These are the ways you will reach your customers. Here, you should put down your ideas for getting your product or service in front of your target audience. Will you use social media, a website, or physical stores? Maybe you'll leverage email marketing, partnerships, or even a YouTube channel. Your channels are the touchpoints between your customers and your brand. Never forget.

- **Customer relationships:** This section focuses on the type of relationship you want to build with your customers. Will you be assisting them personally or giving them access to automated services? A luxury brand, for instance, might go for personal shopping assistants, while an online software company might rely more on automated help desks and user communities.

- **Revenue streams:** This refers to how your business makes money. It could be through direct sales, subscription fees, leasing, licensing, or advertising. If you had a mobile app, you could make money through in-app purchases or a subscription model.

- **Key activities:** This section lists the most crucial things your business must do to be productive. These activities would include manufacturing products, marketing, customer service, or even research and development. For an online retailer, key activities might include managing inventory, processing orders, and handling customer service inquiries.

- **Key resources:** These are the assets you need to create value. They could be physical resources like a store or equipment, intellectual resources like patents or brand names, human resources like skilled employees, or financial resources like cash or credit. You should identify these resources to ensure you have everything necessary to deliver on your value proposition.

- **Key partnerships:** Typically, these are suppliers, strategic alliances, advertising partners or any external companies (or individual) you need to work with to help your business model succeed. Partnerships of this kind can help you leverage other companies' strengths, reduce risk, access new markets, or all of the above.

- **Cost structure:** These are the necessary costs as they relate to your business model. Costs can be fixed, like rent and salaries, or variable, like shipping and production costs.

BMCs have the potential to help you think critically about each aspect of your business and how they all fit together. You'd be surprised at how much clarity it can bring to your entrepreneurial adventure.

How to Set Realistic Milestones and Measure Progress

You've got a grand vision, and the thought of finally sharing it with the world sends shivers down your spine. Exciting is one way to describe what you're feeling. But "overwhelming" is also a top contender.

It's natural, as an entrepreneur with big dreams, to go down the worry spiral trying to make sure you're on the right track. To stay sane, consider setting milestones for your journey. This could mean the difference between having a big win after seven years and having a reason to celebrate every month until you get to the big win (the latter describes milestones). The best way to create milestones is by:

1. Defining the scope

What's the ultimate goal of your business? Your grand vision lies at the final destination. But to get there, you must start by identifying the smaller tasks necessary to achieve the main objective of your business. What needs to be done to get closer to your big dream?

1. Prioritizing tasks

Rule number two of creating milestones: Some tasks are more equal than others. You've got some that must be done first. Then, there are some that can wait. Prioritizing helps you focus on what's most important and ensures you're using your time effectively.

Something else to think about is the dependencies between tasks. If you study your business operations, you'll find tasks that can't be started until others are completed. With this knowledge, you should make a logical sequence of all the tasks completed by your team.

1. Assigning resources

This simply means figuring which teammate will shoulder certain tasks. Prudently give tasks to your team members, taking note of what they can do and their availability. In this way, you'll be sure that each task will be done efficiently. It'll also give you an estimate of how much time each milestone will require. You might have guessed, at this point, that this step works if you have a team. As a solo entrepreneur, use this period to determine the best ways to manage your own time and skills.

1. Setting timelines

Timelines give you a clear sense of direction and help you stay on course. But to get this result, you have to be realistic about how much can be done within a given timeframe. It's better to give yourself a bit of extra time and finish early than to rush and miss deadlines. Try to anticipate potential obstacles and build in some buffer time for unexpected delays.

1.   Monitoring and adjusting

Unlike milestones for a physical journey, the ones you set for your business can be adjusted. This is why you should regularly review your progress. Stay vigilant and keep an eye on how things are going. Are you hitting your deadlines? Are tasks being completed as planned? If something isn't working, be ready to sacrifice it for the good of the ultimate goal.

Inspiring Story

Caroline and Isabel Bercaw

These sisters from Minneapolis, 11 and 12 years old at the time they became entrepreneurs, were avid athletes, constantly looking for ways to soothe their sore muscles after grueling sports practices. They often turned to bath bombs for relief, but the products on the market were simply disappointing. Many left behind messy stains and required a second shower to clean up. Dissatisfied, they made up their minds to do something about it. With a "loan" of $150 from their mother, they set out to create a better, more sustainable bath bomb.

From the grand workstation of their kitchen, they mixed various ingredients, tweaking their formula until they found the perfect balance. The sisters wanted their bath bombs to be, of course, soothing, but also clean and fun. After countless trials and errors, they finally created a product they were proud of. And so, Da Bomb Fizzers was born.

The response from the market was overwhelmingly positive. They sold out of their entire stock on the first day. With their minds blown by success, they spent the entire night making more bath bombs. The next day, they sold out again. It was clear they had hit on something special.

By 2015, Da Bomb Fizzers had made its way into 30 local shops! But there's something quite intentional at play here. What sets the sisters' business apart are the surprises they included inside each bath bomb. Some people found charms, coins, or other trinkets inside their items. This element of surprise has been a hit with customers of all ages.

Today, Da Bomb Fizzers is a thriving company with more than $20 million in annual revenue (Quezada, 2017).

Refining Your Business Ideas

Getting a great idea is like finding a shiny nugget of gold. You can see its amazing potential, but it's still a bit rough and covered in dirt. Before you show it off to the world, you'll want to clean it up and make it as awesome as possible. Just like gold needs to be melted and refined, your ideas need some polishing too. Here's how you can do that.

Be Curious

Curiosity is one of the most powerful engines that drives innovation and growth. This habit—constantly asking questions and seeking new opportunities—can open up a world of possibilities and lead to breakthroughs in your business ideas.

Develop Tolerance for Failure

Know this: It's not the failure itself, but how you respond to it that matters. Those with a high tolerance for failure find it relatively easy to bounce back stronger and smarter if they fall.

Keep an Open Mind

This allows you to see opportunities where others might see obstacles. In fact, you should seek feedback from a variety of sources, including friends, family, teachers, and even strangers. Each person, with their unique experiences and understanding, can give you a different viewpoint that might spark a new idea or help you refine an existing one.

Experiment

Create prototypes, run small tests, and gather data. You've got to be brave and try out some of your ideas if you want to discover what works best for your business.

When you're sure you've nailed a sellable version of your idea, the next riddle to solve is the market. Will people love your polished gold or not? The next chapter discusses strategies for carving out your own piece of the market.

Recommended Reads

The Lean Startup by Eric Ries.

- This book introduces the concept of lean startup methodology, emphasizing iterative development, validated learning, and rapid experimentation. It guides entrepreneurs on how to build a sustainable business by continuously adapting and improving their products or services.

Zero to One by Peter Thiel

- Peter Thiel, co-founder of PayPal and an influential investor, shares insights on creating groundbreaking startups. He encourages entrepreneurs to focus on creating unique, monopoly-like businesses rather than trying to find their place in overcrowded markets.

Chapter 3:

The Magic of Market Research

You can't really have a business without making sales, right? And trying to sell something without any customers just doesn't make sense. So, to make your business work, you need customers. But not just any customer will do. You need the right ones, your target audience. You need to know who they are and where to find them.

Fortunately, there are some fun and effective methods you can employ to locate your audience.

(Complete Worksheet Part 1: Understanding Your Target Audience)

Use Movie Characters to Your Advantage

This might sound a little puppet master-ish at first, but give it a minute, and you might begin to see its merits.

So, filmmakers use characters to tell stories. They are able to establish a deep connection by creating characters that their audience can sympathize with, worry about, and root for. For entrepreneurial purposes, you can humanize your customers using a version of this strategy.

For your movie character, think of your ideal customer. What kind of personality do they have? What are their likes and dislikes?

Consider their background, motivations, and even the types of friends they might have. If you're targeting other teenagers, you might think of characters from popular teen movies. Are your ideal customers more like Katniss Everdeen from *The Hunger Games*, or Hermione Granger from *Harry Potter*? This exercise in creativity can help you strategize where to best communicate with your audience.

(Complete Worksheet Part 2: Audience Avatar Creation)

Observe. Observe. Observe.

Another powerful method is to pay close attention to your audience's behavior. For real, stalk them to discover how they interact with your brand and similar businesses.

You want to know what products or services they most frequently buy? What times of the day or week do they make these purchases? These are important questions you must answer to get a picture of your customer base.

Observation also helps uncover implicit assumptions you might have about your customers. You might assume, for example, that your audience prefers one type of product, but observing their behavior could reveal that they're actually more interested in something else entirely. As an upcoming entrepreneur, the thought of losing money this way should give you the heebie-jeebies!

Social Media Analytics

If you've ever wondered why some posts blow up while others don't even make a sound, social media analytics is your answer. It involves collecting, analyzing, and interpreting data from social media platforms. You might discover that your followers engage most with your educational content, especially when it's related to tips and tricks in your niche, simply by looking at your analytics. With this insight, you may choose to focus more on creating similar content to keep your audience hooked.

Page Views

Page views are exactly what they sound like—the number of times a page on your website is viewed. This metric gives you a sense of which pages are the most popular. If you notice that certain pages are getting a lot of views, that's a clue that your audience is really feeling the content on those pages.

Bounce Rate

Bounce rate represents the percentage of visitors to your website who jump ship after viewing one page. A high bounce rate might indicate that visitors aren't finding what they expected, or that the page isn't engaging enough to keep them interested. A low bounce rate, on the other hand, suggests that visitors are exploring more of your site.

Conversion Rate

Conversion rate measures the percentage of visitors who complete a desired action-filling out a contact form, for instance. If your conversion rate is lower than you'd like, it might be time to tweak your call-to-actions or streamline the user journey to make it easier for visitors to convert.

Likes and Reactions

Today, likes and reactions are the commonest and simplest forms of engagement. They show that your audience appreciates your content and finds it interesting or entertaining.

Tactics for Conducting Market Research

Active Tools

Surveys and Questionnaires

Surveys and questionnaires are some of the most effective tools for conducting market research among teens. They allow you to gather a wide range of data, from product preferences to buying behaviors.

When designing surveys or questionnaires for teens, make sure they're relevant and meaningful. Use casual language that your audience finds relatable. Think about how you speak with the people you're cool with—that's the tone you should aim for. Instead of complicated scales, use a smiley face scale for sentiment ratings. This makes the questions intuitive and fun to answer. For example:

1. How do you feel about our new product?

(smiley face) Love it

(bland) It's okay

(sad emoji) Not for me

Getting your survey out to the right people is just as important as designing it well. Distribute your surveys among your peers or your target audience. There are several ways to do this:

- In person: Hand out printed surveys at school events, clubs, or gatherings.

- Email: If you have access to email lists, this can be an effective way to reach out.

- Social media: Share your survey link in your bio, posts, or stories. Social media, in particular, is a powerful tool. Teens are always online, and a catchy post or story can quickly spread your survey far and wide.

Once you've gathered the responses, it's time to study the data. Look for patterns and trends in the answers. What do most people like? What do they dislike? Use this information to gain insights into your audience's preferences. If you notice that a large number of respondents prefer a specific type of product or service, that's a strong indicator of where to focus your efforts.

Focus Groups

Focus groups are basically hangouts where you and a bunch of others chat about specific stuff—like what makes a game totally epic or why a new phone app rocks your world.

These groups are a blast because everyone gets to share their thoughts, bounce ideas off each other, and see what clicks. You get to hear different perspectives and discover what people really dig (or don't dig) about things.

Companies set up focus groups when they've got a killer idea and want to know what real people think. Say you're in one of these groups testing a custom sneaker design. You and other sneaker enthusiasts geek out over what makes it awesome—like the unique style, comfort features, or innovative materials that make it stand out. That's what it's about.

Ethnographic Research

Unlike focus groups, which are like lively group chats, ethnographic research is all about quietly observing and soaking in the vibes. You'd be learning the secret sauce of what makes people tick without them even realizing it. You get to see the real-life habits and quirks that shape how people interact with things.

This sneaky spy work is ideal when entrepreneurs want to go deep into understanding why people do what they do.

Online Tools

Google Forms and SurveyMonkey are two among many online tools that allow you to design, distribute, and analyze surveys all in one place. They also automatically compile the data, which provides you with easy-to-read charts and graphs to help interpret the results.

Passive Tools

Social Media Listening

This means tracking and analyzing conversations about your brand and industry on social media platforms. You should be tuned into these discussions if you want to get actionable insights about how your brand is perceived. You might see, for instance, a lot of buzz on Instagram about a specific color or style. And after monitoring hashtags and comments, you notice that everyone loves neon-colored sneakers. You can use this insight to create a new line of neon custom sneakers that you know will be a hit.

Collecting Product Reviews

Collecting reviews from online sources gives you direct feedback on your products. They show you what customers love and what needs improvement. You can analyze the common themes you observe to improve the quality of your products and meet customer needs better.

Online Communities and Forums

Online communities and forums are where people talk about their interests. These platforms are full of discussions about products, brands, and trends. Lurking in these communities is useful information about customer pain points, preferences, and new trends. If you join a forum for sneaker enthusiasts, you can see what people are saying about custom sneakers. Maybe there's a trend for eco-friendly materials or a desire for more unique designs. You can learn so much by paying attention to these discussions and possibly even interacting.

The Importance of Market Research

- Understand customer behavior: Market research can help you get into your customers' heads. You can create products and services that they actually want simply by figuring out their likes, dislikes, and needs.

- Evaluate risks: Market research lets you see the lay of the land before you enter a new market or launch a product. It helps you understand the current market conditions and predict how your product will do. This way, you avoid nasty surprises and have a plan to tackle any challenges.

- Concept validation: If you have a cool new idea, you can tell you if it's worth pursuing by researching the market. You can test your concept with real people to see if there's genuine interest and demand. This saves you time and money by avoiding ideas that won't fly and focusing on those that will.

- Identify market gaps: Market research helps you spot what's missing in the market. These gaps are opportunities for you to come in and provide something new and needed. If your competitors have overlooked something, you can swoop in and fill that gap.

- Problem-solving: If you notice any problems with existing products or brands in your industry, market research can help you understand these issues better and find ways to solve them. You can then improve your offerings and attract customers who are dissatisfied with what's currently available.

- Spot opportunities: Market research opens your eyes to opportunities for new products or services that you hadn't thought of before. This could be based on emerging trends, new technologies, or changing consumer preferences.

- Strengthen position: Knowing the market inside out helps you improve your position. You can identify your strengths and weaknesses compared to competitors and work on improving your unique selling points. This makes your brand stronger and more appealing to customers.

- Risk minimization: Every business move has its risks, but market research can help you minimize them. With an understanding of the market and potential pitfalls, you can develop strategies to avoid or mitigate risks.

- Customer-centric approach: Market research puts your customers at the heart of your strategy. You can create products and marketing campaigns that they like if you focus on their needs and preferences. And this is almost impossible with an investment in deep market research.

(Complete Worksheet Part 4: Market Research Analogy: The Pizza Party Method)

Inspiring Story

Alex

This is the story of Alexandra "Alex" Scott, a young girl whose life, though brief, left an indelible mark on the world.

She was born on January 18, 1996, a bundle of joy to her parents, Liz and Jay Scott. But only a few days to her first birthday, Alex learned that she had neuroblastoma, a type of cancer that primarily affects young children. This devastating news could have dampened the spirits of any family, but the Scotts soldiered on. They were determined to support their daughter, and this they did.

When Alex was four years old, she made a decision that would change her life and the lives of countless others. After a stem cell transplant, she told her parents she wanted to host a lemonade stand at the front of the house. Her goal was to raise money to help other kids battling cancer. It was a moment of clarity and purpose that transcended her tender age. In July 2000, Alex's first lemonade stand was set up, and to everyone's astonishment, it raised over $2,000 for pediatric cancer research.

Alex nailed it with her lemonade stand by using some smart market research. She noticed that lemonade stands were a fun and popular activity, so she knew people would be excited to get involved. She was able to get tons of support and participation by learning what her community liked and wanted. Her knack for knowing what would click with people was a big reason why her fundraising efforts were such a huge success.

The success of her first stand made her realize that her small act of kindness had the potential to make a significant impact. Every year, she continued to hold lemonade stands, each time gathering more support and raising more funds. Alex's determination and passion were contagious. Her story spread, inspiring friends, family, and even strangers to join her cause.

By the summer of 2004, Alex had set a more ambitious goal for herself: She wanted to raise $1 million to conduct research for cancer. Despite her worsening health, she remained committed to her mission. In July of that year, just ten days before she tragically left this world, Alex fulfilled her dream.

Her parents were inspired by their daughter's unyielding spirit and founded Alex's Lemonade Stand Foundation (ALSF) in 2005. The foundation's mission was to continue funding research to find better treatments and cures for childhood cancer. To date, the foundation has raised over $200 million for childhood cancer research.

You now have a clear idea of how to set up the framework for your business. In the next chapter, we'll analyze strategies to make sure you have the best possible product or service for the market (Prouty, 2022).

(Complete Worksheets Part 5 – Part 7)

Recommended Reads

Brands Laid Bare: Using Market Research for Evidence-Based Brand Management by Jenni Romaniuk.

- This book explores how market research can inform brand management decisions. It emphasizes evidence-based strategies to build and sustain successful brands.

Asking Questions: The Definitive Guide to Questionnaire Design by Norman M. Bradburn, Seymour Sudman, and Brian Wansink.

- Focused on questionnaire design, this book provides practical guidance for creating effective survey questions. It covers various aspects of survey research, from wording to response options.

The Magic of Market Research

Part 1: Understanding Your Target Audience

Objective: Market research starts with knowing who your customers are! Let's have some fun discovering your target audience.

Instructions: Answer the following questions to start understanding the people who might be interested in your business. Think of them like detectives gathering clues! 🕵️ 🔍

1. Who do you think your customers are?
(Are they teens? Kids? Adults? List them here!)

_____

_____

_____

2. Where do your customers hang out? (Think about online spaces, social media, schools, sports teams, etc.)

_____

_____

_____

The Magic of Market Research

Part 2: Audience Avatar Creation

Objective: Create an Audience Avatar—a fictional character representing your perfect customer! This will help you think like your customer.

Instructions: Fill in the details to create your ideal customer.

---

1. Name: What's the name of your ideal customer?

_____

---

2. Age Group: How old are they?
(Are they teens like you? Older? Younger?)

_____

---

3. Interests and Hobbies: What does your avatar love to do in their free time?

_____

---

4. Biggest Problem: What problem does your avatar need solving?

_____

---

5. Where do they spend time online? (TikTok? Instagram? YouTube?)

_____

WORKSHEET
The Magic of Market Research

Part 3: TeenFriendly Market Research Tool

Objective: Learn simple, fun ways to research the market without needing expensive tools or boring surveys. These methods are teen-tested and teen-approved!

Instructions: Pick one or more tools below to try out.

Instagram Polls: Use Instagram's poll feature in your stories to ask your followers what they think of your idea. Example questions:

- "Would you buy a healthy snack box after school?"
- "What's your favorite type of snack?"

Google Forms: Create a quick survey and send it to your friends or schoolmates. Ask questions like:

- "What's your biggest frustration when finding a good snack?"
- "How much would you pay for a snack box?"

Peer Interviews: Interview your classmates or friends. Use these questions to guide your chat:

- "What's something you wish existed to make your day easier?"
- "Would you use a service that delivers healthy snacks to your school?"

The Magic of Market Research

Part 4: Market Research Analogy: The Pizza Party Method

Analogy: : Market research is like planning a pizza party for your friends. 🍕🎉
You need to know what kind of pizza everyone likes before you order!
If you don't ask your friends what they prefer, you might have many pizzas
no one wants. 🍕

STEP 1:	Ask what they want (Research!).
STEP 2:	Make a plan based on their preferences (Use the data!).
STEP 3:	Deliver the proper pizza (Offer a product people love!).

Takeaway: Market research helps you figure out exactly what your customers
want so you can deliver the perfect "pizza"—or product! 🍕

The Magic of Market Research

Part 5: The Feedback Loop

Objective: After researching, it's time to analyze what you've learned! Let's create a feedback loop to improve your business idea based on what your potential customers say.

Instructions: Fill in the following questions to analyze your research results.

> **1. What did most people say about your idea?**
>
> _____

> **2. Did they have any concerns or things they didn't like?** (Example: "They thought the price was too high.")
>
> _____

> **3. What improvements can you make to your idea based on the feedback?** (Example: "I'll make my snack boxes cheaper and more customizable.")
>
> _____

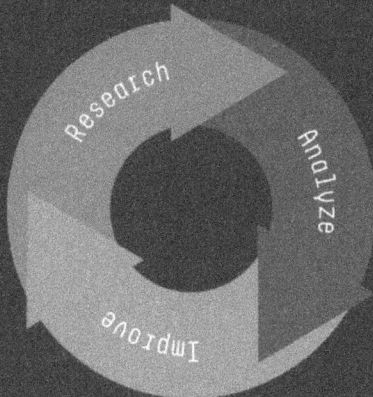

Research

Analyze

Improve

My Market Research Plan

Part 6: Plan Your Questions & Audience!

Objective: Create a simple, step-by-step market research plan to gather feedback on your business idea.

Instructions: Fill in your market research plan below.

1. What do I want to learn from my market research? (Example: "Do teens want to buy customizable snack boxes after school?")

_____

2. Who will I ask? (List your target audience: friends, classmates, online followers, etc.)

_____

3. Which method will I use? (Instagram polls, surveys, interviews, etc.)

_____

4. What three questions will I ask?

1. _____

2. _____

3. _____

The Magic of Market Research

Part 7: Next Steps

Objective: Time to take action and do your market research! What's your next step?

Instructions: Write down what you'll do next to start gathering valuable feedback.

In the next week, I will...

_____

_____

_____

_____

_____

What do I need to do to make this happen? (Example: "Create a Google Form survey and send it to my classmates.")

_____

_____

_____

_____

Chapter 4:

From Brainstorm to Business: Building Your Dream Product/Service

Building a beta (unfinished) version of a product after spending considerable time dreaming up the idea, researching, and refining it, might sound like an extra hassle, but it's super important. It helps you figure out if your idea actually works the way you think it will. There's ageless wisdom in testing the waters before going full body into the river.

Let's say, for whatever reason, you didn't test the waters. You've just designed a pair of custom sneakers, and everything looks perfect on paper. But once you start making them, you might find out that the materials don't work well together, or maybe the design isn't as comfortable as you imagined. The time and money you'd have wasted is as disastrous as skipping the brainstorming process. With a prototype, like a sample pair of sneakers, you can try out your ideas in real life, spot any issues, and make changes to get them just right.

Now, if your idea is really groundbreaking, you'll probably want to protect it with a patent. Here again, you'll need a prototype to get a clear picture of what's truly important about your invention. This can help you design a better patent application. But that's pretty advanced stuff, and for most of you, this isn't something you need to worry about.

One of the greatest benefits of prototypes is how they help with communication. Trying to explain a complex idea to someone using just words or drawings is tough. But if you have a prototype, you can show them exactly what you're talking about. This makes it so much easier to get your team, investors, or any other stakeholders on board. They can see and interact with your concept, which makes it real for them. When people can see what you're aiming for, they'll be more likely to support you and give you valuable feedback.

(Complete Worksheet Step 1: Assessing Your Idea)

Simple Methods for Creating a Prototype

Creating a beta version of your product or service doesn't have to be expensive or overly complicated. In fact, with the right approach and tools, you can develop a good prototype with little money. Here's how.

Use Free or Low-Cost Tools

You may not have to invest in expensive software or equipment when you're just starting. There are many free or low-cost tools available that can help you create prototypes. Keep in mind that this depends on your chosen industry. Some businesses may have a high startup cost, no matter how prudent you are.

Taking note of the complexity of your product, you might be able to create a basic prototype using materials you already have. A DIY approach can save you a lot of money and still give you a tangible version of your idea.

For instance, if you're designing custom sneakers, you can use materials like synthetic suede and rubber outsoles to create a prototype. These materials are easy to find and work with. Even for fashion designs, using fabric swatches, thread, and a sewing machine can help you create your first sample without spending a lot of money.

This merely gives you an idea of how resourceful you can be.

Use Compatible Material Alternatives

For instance, if your final product will be made of metal, you could use plastic or wood for your prototype. These materials are generally cheaper and easier to work with. They can also give you a good sense of the product's dimensions and ergonomics without breaking the bank.

Outsource to a Prototyping Service

While there is a cost associated with services like Protolabs or local fabrication shops for physical products, they do bring expertise and specialized equipment that can save you time and money in the long run. This option is particularly useful for complex products that require precise manufacturing techniques.

As a young entrepreneur, chances are that your business might be service-based rather than product-based. If you're rendering a service, your prototype might involve a detailed service blueprint. You could also conduct a small-scale trial of your service with a few customers.

Prototyping takes a different form for online products. You might use wireframing tools to create a visual representation of your website or app, or develop a Minimum Viable Product (MVP) to test your core features, which is a simplified version of your product that includes just the core features necessary to gather user feedback and test your idea.

(Complete Step 2: Building Your Prototype or Beta Version)

How to Gather Feedback on the Prototype

You can never have too much feedback. As we saw in the previous chapters, constructive criticism is helpful during the brainstorming process of your entrepreneurial journey. And as soon as your prototype is ready, it's feedback time again.

You can gather insights from friends, family, and potential users to help you refine your idea and ensure it meets the needs and expectations of those who will eventually use it. This is how to go about it.

Ask the Right Way

You might be hesitant to get feedback, but chances are your beta testers are hesitant to give you their opinions as well. There are ways to make the process easy for them.

- If you have several versions of your prototype, why not test all of them? Letting people know there's more than one option can be a kind of encouragement for those who feel squeamish about giving harsh criticism.

- You can also use the "I Like, I Wish, What If" technique. This method encourages people to tell you what they like about your prototype, what they wish was different, and what they think could improve it.

(Complete Step 3: Gathering Feedback)

Test Your Prototypes on the Right People

Early in your design process, it might be enough to get some quick thoughts from your friends or family. They can give you initial impressions and help you catch any obvious issues. However, as you move forward and your prototype becomes more polished, you'll need to test it on a representative sample of your target audience.

If your prototype is an educational app for high school students, try to get feedback from actual high school students rather than just adults. If it's a new kitchen gadget, get feedback from people who cook regularly.

Ask the Right Questions

The quality of the feedback you receive depends a lot on the questions you ask. Savvy entrepreneurs typically go for open-ended questions because they encourage detailed responses and insights. Instead of asking, "Do you like this feature?" try asking, "What do you think about this feature?" or "How would you improve this feature?" Avoid leading questions that might bias their answers, like "Don't you think this feature is great?"

Here are a few more examples of good questions to ask:

- What was your first impression of the prototype?

- Was there anything confusing or unclear?

- Can you describe how you would use this in your daily life?

Be Neutral When You Present Your Ideas

Don't try to convince your testers that your prototype is perfect or explain why you made certain design choices right away. Instead, just listen. You want to understand their perspective, not defend your work. If someone doesn't like a part of your prototype, don't take it personally. This is your chance to make it better. Thank them for their honesty and think about how you can address the issues they pointed out.

Say you've designed a cool pair of sneakers, but it's still just a prototype. Then, you let your friends and some potential customers try them out and provide feedback. Some might love the style but think they're uncomfortable, while others might suggest different colors. Then, you let people play with your new thing, you get valuable insights that can help you move forward wisely. For your sneaker business, this means you're not just guessing what will sell—you have real input from real people. This makes your final product more likely to succeed because it's been shaped by the very people who will buy it.

(Complete Steps 4 - 5)

Recommended Reads

The Magic by Rhonda Byrne.

- *The Magic* by Rhonda Byrne reveals a life-changing secret: The power of gratitude can transform all aspects of our lives, including relationships, health, and finances. Through a 28-day journey, readers practice gratitude, leading to a profound shift in perspective and experiences.

The Magic of Thinking Big by David Schwartz.

- This book illustrates that success doesn't require exceptional intelligence or uniqueness. By thinking big, you can motivate yourself to improve your work life, earn more money, and find happiness and fulfillment.

From Brainstorm to Business:

Building Your Dream Product/Service

STEP 1: Assessing Your Idea

Before you can turn your idea into reality, let's evaluate it based on three key factors: market needs, your personal interest, and feasibility.

Instructions: Answer the following questions to assess your business idea.

1. **Does your product or service solve a real problem?**
   (Example: "My snack box solves the problem of not having healthy options after school.")

   _____

2. **Are you passionate about this idea?**
   (Can you see yourself working on this for the next year or more?)

   _____

3. **Is it feasible?**
   (Do you have the resources, skills, or time to build a prototype or provide this service?)

   _____

From Brainstorm to Business:

Building Your Dream Product/Service

STEP 2: Building Your Prototype or Beta Version

Creating a simple version of your product or service helps you see how it works. Don't worry about perfection–focus on creating something that represents your idea.

Instructions: Pick one method to create a prototype or beta version of your product or service.

1. DIY Prototype:

Create a basic version using the materials you have. (For example, Create sample snack boxes, mock up your website, or offer a simplified version of your

What will your DIY prototype look like?

_____

2. Digital Prototype:

Use free tools like Canva or Wix to make a mock-up or digital version of your product or service.

Which tool will you use for your prototype?

_____

3. Beta Version of Your Service:

Offer your service to a small group of people for free or at a discount to test it out.

What is your service beta plan?

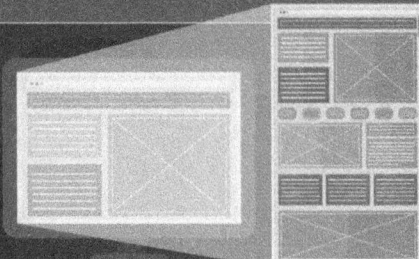

_____

From Brainstorm to Business:

Building Your Dream Product/Service

STEP 3: Gathering Feedback

Feedback is essential to improving your product or service. Be open to listening, especially to constructive criticism, as it will help improve your business!

Instructions: Select five people to try out your prototype or beta version and ask for their honest opinions.

1. What do you like the most about this product/service?

_____

2. What could be improved?

_____

3. Would you use this product/service again? Why or why not?

_____

Who will you ask for feedback?

_____   _____

_____   _____

_____

From Brainstorm to Business:

Building Your Dream Product/Service

STEP 4: Improving Your Product Based on Feedback

Now that you've gathered feedback, it's time to make improvements. Remember, even the best products start with rough drafts!

Instructions: Use the feedback you gathered to list three changes or improvements you can make to your product or service.

1. What's the most significant change you'll make?

_____

2. What minor tweaks can you make to improve the user experience?

_____

3. What's one bold change you're considering after getting feedback?

_____

From Brainstorm to Business:

Building Your Dream Product/Service

STEP 5: Next Steps to Launch

You've built a prototype, gathered feedback, and made improvements—now it's time to think about what's next!

Instructions: Write down three things you will do next to continue building and launching your business.

1. _____
2. _____
3. _____
4. _____

Chapter 5:

Building Your Support Group

Mentors can be the guiding light you need to survive the journey to become an entrepreneur. They can provide you with invaluable advice, share their experiences, and support you with their network and funds.

How to Find Mentors

To find the support you need, you'll have to get involved in networking. But let's be real—most teens aren't going to walk into a networking event at the Hyatt and just start mingling. So, how do you find venues appropriate for teens?

You can begin by asking your mom and dad to help connect you with people they know who are in similar businesses. They might have friends or colleagues who can help you with valuable advice or introductions. Also, many colleges have incubator programs specifically for teens. These programs often host networking events or workshops where you can meet other young entrepreneurs and learn from experienced businesspeople. Check out local colleges to see what they offer.

Look for events that are centered on specific types of businesses. Some startup incubators and co-working spaces host presentations from vendors that you might need as a startup. These are great opportunities to learn and network. Don't be shy—

engage in conversations, introduce yourself, and express your entrepreneurial interests. Be genuine and enthusiastic about your experiences. You never know who you might meet—maybe someone with extensive experience who understands your vision and is willing to help.

As you prepare for these events, work on your elevator pitch. This is a brief, engaging introduction about yourself and your business idea. To develop a strong pitch, start with who you are, what your business does, and why it's unique. Practice it until you can deliver it confidently and naturally. This will help you make a memorable first impression.

Cities with thriving startup scenes often have entrepreneurial hotspots like startup incubators, co-working spaces, and innovation hubs. These places are bustling with activity and are home to many innovators. Spend time in these environments to immerse yourself in the entrepreneurial culture.

In these hot spots, you'll meet individuals who have walked the path you are just starting on. They understand the challenges and triumphs of entrepreneurship. Engage with them and ask questions. These interactions can lead to valuable relationships with potential mentors who can provide insights and support as you build your business.

Remember, after meeting new contacts, follow up with a thank-you email or connect on professional networking sites like LinkedIn. This suggests that you value their time and are serious about building a relationship.

Other places to connect with mentors include:

- The internet: Websites like SCORE.org, SBA.gov, and TeenBizBootcamp have mentorship programs specifically designed for young entrepreneurs. These platforms connect entrepreneurs like you with experienced business professionals who are eager to share their knowledge.

Social media platforms like LinkedIn and Twitter are also excellent tools for connecting with industry experts.

- Schools and universities: Many schools and universities have resources dedicated to supporting young entrepreneurs. They often make entrepreneurship clubs, incubators, and dedicated advisors available to students. If you're a student, take advantage of these opportunities. Usually, schools also have networks of alumni who are successful entrepreneurs and are willing to mentor current students. You can leverage these connections for your entrepreneurial growth.

- Local business scene: Your local business community is another great place to find mentors. Reach out to local business owners and entrepreneurs, and ask if they would be willing to meet for coffee to discuss your business idea. These informal meetings can lead to valuable connections and potential mentorship opportunities.

- Small Business Development Centers (SBDCs): These are independent organizations that provide resources, expertise, and advice to emerging entrepreneurs. They can furnish you with free consultations and connect you with experienced business advisors. SBDCs are a fantastic resource for young entrepreneurs who could do with some much-needed guidance. They organize workshops, one-on-one mentoring sessions, and provide access to a network of business professionals. Locate an SBDC near you and take advantage of this support. The advice and insights you gain can be instrumental in the success of your business.

- Incubators, accelerators, and co-working spaces: These environments are designed to support startups and give them access to a community of successful entrepreneurs, mentors, and industry experts. Incubators and accelerators also often have structured programs that include mentorship, funding opportunities, and networking events.

- Local Chamber of Commerce: Your local Chamber of Commerce is an organization that supports local businesses and exists to champion economic growth. They, too, host networking events, business seminars, and community initiatives, and you can connect with successful business owners and professionals at these events. The relationships you build through the Chamber of Commerce can help you with the support and guidance you need to thrive as a young entrepreneur.

Green Flags to Look for in Mentors

As we acknowledged in the section above, mentors can be valuable assets in your entrepreneurial adventure. They can keep you from making serious mistakes and share some of their strengths with you—including their connections and money. But, sadly, not all mentors are cut from the same cloth. Many of them can actually be disadvantageous to the realization of your dreams. As such, you should be aware of potential red flags that could indicate a less-than-ideal mentorship relationship.

Here's what you should look for in a good mentor:

- Active listener: A great mentor listens to you. They value your ideas and concerns and don't interrupt or disregard what you have to say. An active listener can give you truly helpful advice that's relevant to your situation. So, if you find a mentor who listens carefully, you've struck gold.

- Respectful and supportive: Respect is key. Your mentor should treat you and your ideas with respect, encouraging you to grow and build confidence. If they belittle your ideas or talk down to you, it's a sign they might not be the

80

right fit. Look for someone who builds you up and supports your journey.

- Clear communicator: Good communication is crucial. Your mentor should be able to explain things clearly, engage in open and honest discussions, and ensure you're both on the same page. Misunderstandings can derail your progress, so a mentor who communicates well is essential.

- Focused on you: While personal stories can be inspiring, a mentor who constantly veers into unrelated personal matters might not be as committed to your professional growth. Your mentorship time should be about your development and goals, so look for someone who keeps the focus on you.

- Committed and available: Consistency matters. Your mentor should keep regular meetings and show genuine interest in your progress. If they frequently cancel or reschedule, it might be time to reconsider. Regular contact is crucial for continuous support and development.

- Celebrate your success: A good mentor should advocate for your skills and recognize your accomplishments, not take credit for them. They should celebrate your successes and help you shine. If a mentor claims your achievements as their own, it's a major red flag.

- Constructive criticism: Supportive mentors help you learn from mistakes rather than blame you for them. They provide constructive criticism that aids your growth. If they constantly accuse or diminish your efforts, it's not a healthy environment for development.

- Respect your path: Everyone's journey is unique. A mentor should respect your path and not try to remake you in their image. Look for someone who supports your individuality and helps you carve out your own success story.

- Maintain integrity: Your mentor should never push you to compromise your values or ethics. Integrity is crucial in entrepreneurship, and your mentor should respect and support your commitment to ethical practices. If you feel pressured to act against your values, it's a clear sign to move on.

- Respect your autonomy: While guidance is important, you should ultimately make your own decisions. A mentor who tries to control your choices or manipulate you for their own benefit won't help you grow. Seek a mentor who respects your autonomy and encourages you to be the decision-maker.

- Open to feedback: Feedback should go both ways. A good mentor is open to receiving feedback from you and uses it to strengthen the relationship. If your mentor gets defensive or dismissive when you share your thoughts, they might not be the right fit. Mutual respect and a willingness to learn from each other are vital.

Now, don't just stick to one type of mentor. It's beneficial to have mentors from different business areas. This variety provides a broader education and support network, which can help you become a well-rounded entrepreneur. For instance, a financial mentor can guide you on budgeting and investments, while a marketing mentor can help you understand your target audience.

(Complete Step 1: Finding Mentors & Advisors)

(Complete Step 2: How to Approach Potential Mentors)

Success Stories

Kim Bercaw

Kim Bercaw, a devoted mother and astute businesswoman, was super important in nurturing the entrepreneurial spirit of her daughters, Caroline and Isabel Bercaw (remember them?).

Seeing the potential in their daughters' venture, Kim and her husband, Benjamin, made a bold decision. They both quit their day jobs to fully commit to growing Da Bomb Bath Fizzers. This decision wasn't taken lightly. They were letting go of a sure thing to focus on a dream, so this essentially a leap of faith driven by a strong belief in their daughters' vision and the unique product they had created. Kim and Benjamin's unwavering support and dedication became the backbone of the company, allowing Caroline and Isabel to flourish.

Kim took on the responsibility of managing marketing and branding. With her expertise and strategic thinking, she positioned Da Bomb Bath Fizzers in the market, helping it reach a broad audience. She worked tirelessly to create a likable and unmissable brand. Her efforts paid off as the bath bombs found their way into major retail stores like Target and Ulta.

Meanwhile, Benjamin managed the finances and operations, ensuring the company's smooth running. His job was to maintain the business's financial health and scalability. Together, Kim and Benjamin formed a formidable team, each bringing their unique skills to the table.

Kim's role as a mentor was extremely beneficial to her children's vision. She provided the necessary business acumen and guidance, allowing Caroline and Isabel to focus on what they did best—creating and connecting. Kim gave advice to her daughters and empowered them to make decisions, encouraged them to take risks, and helped them learn from their experiences. She nurtured their creativity and entrepreneurial spirit (Scheps, 2021).

Jake Goldblum and Chris Mengel

This is the story of Ryan Draving, a young entrepreneur who found his path to success with the help of two remarkable mentors, Jake Goldblum and Chris Mengel.

Ryan Draving's life took a major turn when he met Jake Goldblum, the President and CEO of Empire Covers. Ryan began working closely with Jake at Empire Covers, taking on the role of his right-hand man. This experience was everything for Ryan, who was then a teenage entrepreneur brimming with ideas but lacking the practical know-how to bring them to fruition.

Jake's leadership style and dedication to his business left a lasting impression on Ryan. Jake demonstrated what it meant to lead with integrity and passion, showing Ryan that true leadership involves a deep commitment to your work and the people you lead.

One major lesson Ryan picked up from Jake was the importance of setting high standards and maintaining a relentless pursuit of excellence. Jake's approach to business was near flawless; he believed in doing things right the first time and never settling for mediocrity. Being in such close proximity to greatness, Ryan began to understand that success in business actually lies in the way a business is executed, and not just in having an idea alone.

In 2012, Ryan's path crossed with another influential mentor, Chris Mengel, at a hackathon. Chris, the founder of RazorWest and Mamook Media, brought a different perspective to Ryan's entrepreneurial goals. Where Jake had taught him the importance of commitment and operational excellence, Chris introduced Ryan to the world of strategic innovation and marketing.

Chris Mengel encouraged Ryan to think outside the box and to be fearless in his pursuit of innovative solutions. He also inspired him to believe in his vision and to take bold steps toward making it come true.

Chris often emphasized that while innovation is crucial, it must be grounded in a solid strategy. And so, he helped Ryan develop a keen sense for identifying market opportunities and creating strategies that leverage these opportunities effectively (Moore, 2014).

(Complete Worksheet Step 3 - 5)

Recommended Reads

A Guide to Running a Mental Health Support Group by Josh Steinberg.

- This guide, specifically designed for OCD support groups, outlines various formats for support groups. It includes insights on effective group formats and their suitability for different member characteristics.

How to Build a Support System for Your Ministry by Roy M. Oswald.

- Roy Oswald offers practical guidance for clergy in developing a peer support system. The book covers starting support groups, the role of facilitators, rituals, finding encouragers, and navigating crises.

Building Your Support Group

STEP 1: Finding Mentors and Advisors

Mentors and advisors can guide you, offer advice, and share their experiences to help you grow. The best part? You can start building your support group as a teen!

Instructions: List the people in your life who could become your mentors or advisors or help connect you to others.

1. Who do you admire?
Think about people you know personally (teachers, coaches, family members) who inspire you and who you'd like to learn from.

_____

2. Who has experience in the field you're interested in?
List people who may already be successful in your area of interest (entrepreneurs, professionals, etc.).

_____

3. Who has offered you support or advice in the past?
Sometimes, mentors are people already in your life who believe in you and want to see you succeed.

_____

Building Your Support Group

STEP 2: How to Approach Potential Mentors

Now that you've identified potential mentors and advisors, it's time to approach them. Don't be afraid to reach out–they were once in your shoes, too!

Instructions: Write down how you'll approach the people you listed above. You can use email, social media, or even a conversation after class. Here's how you can structure your message:

Introduction: Briefly introduce yourself.
Example: "Hi, I'm [Your Name], and I'm really passionate about [your business idea or interest]."

_____

Compliment or Acknowledge their Experience:
Example: "I've always admired how you've built your business, and I'd love to learn from your experience."

_____

Request for advice or mentorship:
Example: "Would you be open to sharing some advice or offering guidance as I develop my idea?"

_____

Building Your Support Group

STEP 3: Expanding Your Network

Networking is an essential skill for building your support group. It's all about connecting with people who can inspire you, help you grow, and open doors for future opportunities. You can start building your network right now!

Instructions: Write down three ways you can expand your network as a teen.

1. Join Clubs or Groups:
Example: Join a school club, community group, or online community related to your interests.

_____

2. Attend Events or Webinars:
Look for events (in person or virtual) where professionals or entrepreneurs share advice.

_____

3. Leverage Social Media:
Use LinkedIn, Instagram, or other platforms to follow and engage with people in your field of interest.

_____

Building Your Support Group

STEP 4: The Power of Networking

Networking isn't just about what people can do for you; it's about building relationships and learning from others. Here are some tips for effective networking as a teen:

Be genuine and curious: Always approach people with a real interest in learning from them, not just asking for favors.

Give as much as you take: Offer to help where you can, even if it's something small like volunteering.

Follow up and stay connected: After meeting someone new, send them a follow-up message and keep in touch.

Reflection:

1. How will you make networking a regular habit in your life?

_____

2. What's one networking opportunity you plan to pursue this month?

_____

Building Your Support Group

STEP 5: Next Steps in Building Your Support Group

It's time to implement your plan and start building your support group!

Instructions: Write down the following three steps you will take to find mentors advisors, and expand your network.

1. _____
2. _____
3. _____
4. _____

Chapter 6:

Bringing Your Vision to Life

In the rush of becoming founders, many budding entrepreneurs hurry to bring their products or services to market without a solid plan in place. You might be a young entrepreneur launching a custom sneaker brand. Your passion for sustainable practices has led you to create innovative designs, but chances are that your initial sales may be lackluster (being a beginner and all). Usually, it's the strategy behind the introduction of the product to the market that's the problem, and not the product itself. Without understanding your target audience's values and preferences, you might miss the mark on branding and marketing. Through detailed planning and a refined execution strategy, you can be a sniper with your brand execution.

Creating a Killer Brand Identity

When I first started my own business, I didn't really take branding seriously. I just didn't understand why this part of building a business was so important. But, as I went through the different phases of launching and scaling the business, it became evident that a strong brand identity can make or break my whole dream! Despite having an innovative product, I wasn't making enough sales. I realized that potential customers didn't just buy what you *sell*. It's not really how human beings operate. Instead, they buy the why of what you're selling.

This epiphany led me down a path where I began defining a brand identity for my business.

So, where do you start? That's the easy part. Begin by answering the question of "who you are and what your business stands for." Reflect on your values, mission, and vision. For me, it was about being environmentally responsible and providing value without compromising quality. You can ask these questions:

- What is my mission?

- What is my vision for the future?

These core principles should shine through in every facet of your brand. With that done, you also want to know your audience. Who are they? What do they care about? What problems do they need solving? Immerse yourself in their world. Learn their language, preferences, and pain points.

Once you have clarity on your brand's essence and audience, it's time to ramp up the fun. Your next mission, if you choose to accept it, is to craft your brand elements. This is where you come up with your name, logo, colors, and tagline. People often start with this part, but that's putting the cart before the horse. Keep in mind that your brand elements should reflect the personality of your business. So, defining the personality of your brand should come first. Now, these elements need to harmonize and convey a unified message across all your platforms—be it your website, social media, or packaging. This means that you should create a consistent story for your business.

In the spirit of storytelling, talk to your audience about the challenges and triumphs you've experienced in the course of building the business. People connect with stories, especially ones that are genuine and relatable. So, engage with your community. Talk to them. Also, remember to listen. Respond to their comments and ask for feedback. This will help you make your story increasingly more relatable.

Something else you should do while building your brand is cultivating partnerships that bring your business in front of more eyes. Carefully seek out influencers, corporate brands, or even causes with whom you can work together. The keyword here is "carefully." Choose partners whose values match yours. This is because sacrificing your authenticity for popularity may hurt your brand in the long run.

For good measure, get tech savvy for your business. If you have the know-how, use data and analytics to perfect your brand strategy. If you don't have this skill, you might want to outsource this task. For your data analysis, pay attention to metrics such as engagement rates, customer reviews, and sales trends. These insights will shine a light on what's working and those areas that might need improvement.

Building Brand Presence Through Social Media

We just mentioned careful planning and execution as crucial parts of your brand strategy. Let's talk some more about that.

If asked about the essence of your brand, you might say it's your logo or slogan. In fact, it's about the experience and emotions that people associate with your product or service. To exceed market expectations, you need to know how people are perceiving your brand and make sure it's mostly positive.

You can use social media to achieve the most beneficial perception for your brand. Once you know your target audience, speak directly to them through social media. Create content *they* find valuable, and not just what you like (although that's important too). Social media platforms have tools like polls, stories, and live videos that help you interact directly with your audience. Use as many as you find relevant to your business. Stay updated on new trends and features, but be cautious not to jump on every bandwagon. Sometimes less is more. Focus on high-quality posts that engage your audience, these are far more effective than numerous lackluster ones.

Since you won't always get it right, be prepared for anything. How you handle negative feedback or a public mistake can impact your reputation. Always address issues calmly and transparently. Make sure your response shows empathy and a willingness to learn and improve.

Final Preparations for Services

Like a chef perfecting a recipe before serving it to diners, the final preparations you make to your brand presence and products are just as important as the early stages. Something as simple as your delivery process can ruin all the work you've put into growing your brand. When your products are brought to your customers, you want the experience to be seamless and enjoyable from start to finish. Keep in mind that first impressions are lasting; hence every aspect of your service has to run smoothly.

Here's what you can do to perfect the delivery process:

- Map out each step from the moment a customer interacts with your business to the point where they've received the service. This could be done through flowcharts or diagrams.

- Identify any potential pain points or areas where customers might face issues. If you were in their shoes, would there be any part of the process that seems confusing or slow?

- Test these processes yourself. Act like a customer and go through each step to see if it truly works as intended. Sometimes, the act of experiencing it firsthand reveals flaws that weren't visible on paper.

When you hire staff, keep in mind that you need to train them on all these same things that you have spent time figuring out. They are the ambassadors of your brand, after all. They should be competent, of course, but their interactions with your customers should correctly reflect the values and mission of your business. With proper training, they'll know exactly how to deliver the best possible experience to your customers.

To get this right, here are some steps you need to take:

- Draft clear, comprehensive training manuals. These should cover everything from company policies to detailed instructions on performing specific tasks.

- Conduct hands-on training sessions. Role-playing different scenarios can be particularly effective. For instance, practice how to handle difficult customers or how to upsell services without being pushy.

- Foster an environment where ongoing learning is encouraged. Regular feedback sessions, workshops, and refresher courses can be utilized to keep your employees' skills sharp.

If you are selling services instead of products, then having the right human touch is all the more important. This is because services often involve direct interactions between staff and customers. Each interaction should be treated as an opportunity to leave a positive impression and turn one-time customers into loyal advocates. Whether you do this right or not, your customers will quite likely give you feedback. You should welcome and encourage this criticism or praise.

Recommended Reads

Bringing Your Vision to Life: By Asking the Unasked Questions by Jasmine Phipps.

- This book shares the author's journey of finding her vision despite life's struggles and obstacles. It guides readers to discover their own vision and take steps toward achieving their dreams and goals.

Permission to Leap: The Six-Phase Journey to Bring Your Vision to Life by Bri Seeley (Foreword by Naveen Jain).

- Bri Seeley outlines a six-phase process for turning your vision into reality. The book provides practical steps and inspiration to help you take the leap toward your dreams.

Chapter 7:

Launching With a Bang

What if your launch could leave an impression so strong that it becomes the talk of the town? The thrill of launching something new lies in its potential to make waves. But how do you turn that potential into reality?

Many young entrepreneurs dive headlong into launches without enough preparation. What often results are missed opportunities, disappointments, and lost money. The third one in that trio of doom might be so bad that it stops your business in its tracks. If you release a groundbreaking app that fails to capture interest, or you put in so much work into organizing an event only for it to fall flat, you might be looking at the loss of a huge part of your capital. Thankfully, these setbacks can be preventable with the right strategy.

Steps for Planning a Successful Launch

Once planning for your launch begins, every decision you make needs to be grounded in solid data. Doing this will give you the best shot at success. How, you ask? Looking at the data, like you did during the brainstorming and branding stages, will be immensely beneficial to the way you communicate during marketing. Each promotional piece should speak directly to your audience's needs and desires, and peeking behind the curtain via data will help you achieve this. A great way to test your marketing communications is by gathering a small group from your target demographic and running your messaging by them. Now, there are a few things you should note when you do this. Did your potential customers get excited? Did they see the value? If the answers are yes, you're on the right track.

Whether it's virtual or in real life, you want your launch to be unforgettable. Think of creative ways to engage your audience. For digital products, try hosting interactive demos or Q&A sessions where people can ask questions and get live answers. If you're launching something physical, like our custom sneaker example or a lawn care service, consider raffles or giveaways. For instance, you could give away a free pair of custom sneakers or offer a free lawn mowing service to a lucky winner. These activities make your launch exciting and help you connect with your audience in a fun way.

Additionally:

- Choose a location (even if virtual) that reflects your brand spirit and appeals to your audience.

- Send out invites early, and make sure to hype up the event in all your communications.

- Have a detailed schedule but don't be too rigid with it. Things may not always go as planned, and being adaptable can save the day.

Now, many seasoned entrepreneurs consider that last point to be an even bigger deal than the others. You want to know where your target audience hangs out most? Since you're a teenager potentially trying to sell to other young people, it might be wise to leverage online platforms and e-commerce solutions over traditional brick-and-mortar stores. Sites like Instagram, TikTok, and Snapchat, as you quite likely know, are powerful tools for businesses hoping to be discovered and close deals.

Also, try these out to develop winning sales channels:

- Set up an easy-to-navigate website where transactions are seamless. The fewer clicks it takes to buy something, the better.

- Explore partnerships with popular e-commerce sites or local retailers who share your brand values.

- Ensure your customer service is top of the line. Happy customers will announce you better than any ad campaign.

All of this sounds like a lot, and it is, but taking them one at a time makes it manageable. Even the best-laid plans will face unexpected challenges. Don't see these as setbacks, but as opportunities to show resilience and adaptability.

To recap, successful launches rely heavily on good planning and grounded strategies:

- **Research your market** to understand your audience deeply.

- **Tailor your communications** to speak directly to them in ways that are engaging and relatable.

- **Host an engaging launch event** that fits your brand vibe.

- **Strategize your sales channels** for maximum reach and ease of purchase.

- **Stay adaptable and transparent**, ready to change your direction when necessary.

- **Monitor and refine** your approach based on real-time feedback and data.

Marketing Strategy and Storytelling

Stories are powerful when they're relatable. They humanize brands and make them memorable. Chances are there's a compelling story behind your favorite brand that drew you in. Maybe it's how a popular shoe company started with two young entrepreneurs making shoes from their garage, or how a coffee shop began with a passion for ethically sourced beans. A good story often involves struggle, triumph, and purpose. Why did you start this business? What problem are you solving? Those are the questions you need to answer.

Be real and authentic. Real stories attract real people. But how do you weave this story into your marketing strategy effectively? First off, it needs to be shared across all platforms in a unified way. Make sure the core message remains unchanged. You might know that consistency builds trust. When people see the same message repeated, it sticks with them. So, take time to think up or brainstorm a compelling narrative you're willing to maintain for a long time.

Also, utilize visuals. Humans are visual creatures; we process images faster than text. Use photos, videos, infographics, and other visual elements to make your story vivid and engaging. If you're talking about a product, show it in use, not just sitting idle. Highlight its benefits through real-life scenarios.

Again, everyone loves a good story, especially when it's told with passion and authenticity. So, share your story consistently, engage with your audience genuinely, and don't shy away from showing your true self. When executed thoughtfully, your marketing strategy won't just launch your business, it'll impact lives far beyond what you initially envisioned.

Pre-Launch Checklist

Okay, so you're all set with your pre-launch prep. Let's double-check everything with a quick checklist before you go live:

- **Mission and vision:** crystal clear and communicated effectively.

- **Audience understanding:** detailed personas created and validated.

- **Product readiness:** thoroughly tested and refined based on feedback.

- **Brand story:** authentic, compelling, and relatable narrative crafted.

- **Visuals:** professional design elements in place.

- **Marketing buzz:** social media and influencer collaborations underway.

- **Website:** user-friendly, informative, and SEO-optimized.

With your checklist confirmed, your launch day should be easy-peasy—relatively speaking. Now let's talk post-launch.

Sometimes, the best insights come after the product is in the hands of real users. So, be prepared to pivot or tweak aspects based on this valuable input. Cultivate a strong community around your brand and treat them with respect. This means you should be responsive and show appreciation for the feedback they give you, whether positive or negative. Address any issues they raise immediately, and communicate openly with your audience about how you're working to improve.

One last thing—don't neglect self-care during this process. Launching a business can be intense, emotionally and physically.

Make sure to balance work with rest and stay connected with your support system. Passion without burnout is the goal.

Inspiring Success Stories

Facebook

In the early 2000s, a young Harvard sophomore named Mark Zuckerberg birthed an idea that would change social media, and the whole world, forever. On February 4, 2004, Zuckerberg launched TheFacebook. It was designed as a platform to connect Harvard students. This relatively simple idea quickly gained traction, marking the beginning of Facebook's meteoric rise.

Before creating Facebook, Zuckerberg had already made a name for himself on campus with a controversial project called FaceMash. This site allowed students to compare photos of their peers and vote on who was more attractive. Although FaceMash was short-lived, it demonstrated Zuckerberg's technical prowess and his understanding of the social dynamics at play in a university setting. Despite facing backlash from the administration and women's groups, the popularity of FaceMash planted a seed in Zuckerberg's mind about the potential for a broader social network.

Throughout his sophomore year, Zuckerberg worked tirelessly on what would become Facebook. He saw in his mind a digital space where students could create profiles, share information, and connect with each other in a more meaningful way. On the day of its launch, Zuckerberg and his roommates were glued to their screens, eagerly watching as their creation went live. Within the first 24 hours, over 1,200 Harvard students had registered. This told them that there was a strong demand for this new form of online interaction.

Zuckerberg and his team quickly expanded the platform to other Boston-area schools, and then to the entire Ivy League. Targeting specific, interconnected communities in this way allowed Facebook to grow rapidly while maintaining a sense of exclusivity and relevance. By the end of 2004, Facebook had reached one million users, an astonishing achievement for a company still in its infancy.

A game-changing moment in Facebook's early history came when Peter Thiel, a prominent angel investor, invested $500,000 in the fledgling company. This investment provided the financial stability needed for Zuckerberg to leave Harvard to focus on Facebook full-time. Relocating the company to California, Zuckerberg and his team were now in the heart of the tech world, ready to take their vision to new heights.

From a little seed sown in college, Facebook evolved into a global social media platform. The company's growth was fueled by its ability to innovate and adapt to the changing needs of its users. Features such as the News Feed, introduced in 2006, radically changed how people consumed and shared information online (Reinstein, 2018).

Airbnb

In 2007, two roommates, Brian Chesky and Joe Gebbia, found themselves struggling to pay their rent. As they pondered their financial dilemma, a unique idea was born. There was a design conference about to happen, but none of the hotels nearby had available rooms. Seizing this opportunity, they decided, for a fee, to give out air mattresses in their apartment to attendees of the conference. They released their website, airbedandbreakfast.com, and provide airbeds and a homemade breakfast for $80 each night. When three people took up their offer, Chesky and Gebbia realized that they were on to something.

Seeing the potential in their idea, another member joined the tribe: Nathan Blecharczyk. Together, they began to develop a business model around their concept. Despite initial setbacks and being neck-deep in debt, the team persevered. They tried a couple of times to launch the business, including during the SXSW 2008 Conference and the 2008 Democratic National Convention in Denver. However, user traction did not follow as expected.

The road to success for these guys was anything but easy. Chesky, Gebbia, and Blecharczyk faced numerous challenges and setbacks. At times, they found themselves on the brink of giving up, but their unwavering belief in their idea kept them going. They worked tirelessly, often surviving on a diet of cereal and maxing out multiple credit cards to keep their dream alive. Their persistence eventually paid off when they received seed funding from Y Combinator. The startup accelerator provided them with the resources and mentorship needed to refine their business model.

Their next defining move came when they decided to shorten their website's name to Airbnb.com. This rebranding was meant to represent an expansion of their vision. No longer limited to airbeds and shared spaces, Airbnb began to provide a wide array of properties. This broadened appeal helped them attract a larger and more diverse user base.

Airbnb's growth was exponential after that. They soon evolved into a global phenomenon—a big leap from the small experiment the business was. The company disrupted the traditional hotel industry by creating a new way for people to travel and experience different cultures.

Pinterest

Pinterest, a visual discovery engine that now boasts over 400 million monthly active users, began with an innovative vision from its founders, Ben Silbermann, Paul Sciarra, and Evan Sharp.

Before Pinterest, the founders had started Cold Brew Labs, a mobile shopping startup. Their first app, Tote, was supposed to be the first woman's fashion catalog on the iPhone. But it wasn't a hit. Despite its lack of success, the founders noticed that users appreciated the feature allowing them to save items. This observation led to the realization that people were sharing their tastes with friends, which sparked the idea of pivoting to a social commerce application. This new concept would make curating and sharing collections of products simple and enjoyable.

Evan Sharp, an architecture student at Columbia University, was introduced to Ben Silbermann through a mutual friend. Although Sharp initially worked at Facebook in product design, he decided to help Silbermann and Sciarra as a side project. Sharp had a personal need to organize thousands of photos and architectural drawings effectively online, which led to his design of a grid layout for images. This grid layout represented a breakthrough digital experience and became a defining feature of Pinterest.

The team devoted months to refining the details of the grid, before they launched the business in March 2010. They continuously improved the platform based on user feedback, until they'd created a unique space where people could discover and save ideas for various projects and interests.

Buffer

Joel Gascoigne's brainchild, Buffer, was designed to help people schedule social media content. This idea was born out of a personal need to space out his tweets and automate the process.

The initial version of Buffer was modest in its capabilities and allowed users to schedule tweets and little more. Despite its simplicity, the platform soon caught on. Within just four days of its launch, Buffer secured its first paying customer. A few weeks into its operation, Buffer's user base had grown to 100. This steady growth was a clear signal that the product was meeting a real need.

Over the next nine months, Buffer's user count skyrocketed to 100,000.

With the product gaining traction, Joel realized that marketing and customer engagement were as important as the development of the tool. The product was "good enough," and it was time to let the world know about it. So, Joel brought on a co-founder to help manage the growing demands of development, marketing, and customer engagement. This made sure that Buffer could continue to evolve while reaching a broader audience.

Today, Buffer stands as one of the most well-known social media management platforms. It serves small businesses, creators, and individuals worldwide. From its humble beginnings, Buffer has grown into a leading platform with a remote team of nearly 90 people.

Adidas

Founded by Adolf "Adi" Dassler in a small town in Bavaria, Germany, Adidas is one of many examples of the merits of starting small. It was in his mother's washroom that Adi started designing and cobbling shoes. In 1924, he registered the "Gebrüder Dassler Schuhfabrik" (Dassler Brothers Shoe Factory) with his brother Rudolf. Adi's mission was to help athletes get the best kits. His dedication to quality and performance quickly gained recognition.

Adi Dassler's strategy for the business was unique and ahead of its time. He wanted to make shoes that athletes loved and, to achieve this, he sought feedback directly from the users of his products— the athletes. He listened to their needs and incorporated their suggestions into his designs. This customer feedback-driven approach allowed Adidas to create products that not only met but exceeded the expectations of its customers. It was this focus on customer satisfaction and continuous improvement that set Adidas apart from its competitors.

Things began to really gather steam in the 1936 Olympics in Berlin, where American athlete Jesse Owens won four gold medals wearing Dassler's spikes. This moment catapulted the brand into the international spotlight. It showcased the effectiveness and superiority of Adi's designs on a global stage. The success of Owens and other athletes wearing Adidas shoes demonstrated the brand's ability to deliver performance-enhancing products, further solidifying its reputation.

Adi Dassler's relentless pursuit of innovation continued to drive the brand forward. He was constantly experimenting with new materials and designs, always looking for ways to improve the performance of his products. This commitment to innovation is evident in some of the groundbreaking products introduced by Adidas over the years. For instance, many agree that the introduction of the screw-in stud for football boots changed the sport. It provided players with better traction and stability.

In the 1950s and 1960s, as television brought sports into people's homes, Adidas capitalized on the growing interest in sports by expanding its product range and increasing its marketing efforts. The iconic three stripes, originally introduced for added shoe stability, became a symbol of quality and performance recognized worldwide.

Today, Adidas continues to lead the way in the sportswear industry.

Mojang

Few stories are as inspiring as that of Mojang Studios and its flagship game, Minecraft. Founded by Markus Persson in 2009, Mojang Studios matched creativity with passion. No wonder they became so successful.

Markus Persson, often known by his online alias "Notch," developed an interest in video games at an early age. By the time he was eight, he had already begun learning to program. This early start allowed Persson to hone his skills and develop a deep understanding of what makes a game enjoyable and engaging.

Minecraft began as a simple sandbox game where players could build structures using textured cubes in a 3D world. The alpha version of the game was released in 2009, and it quickly gained a following among PC gamers. Over the next two years, during its alpha and beta phases, Mojang Studios fine-tuned various aspects of the game and continuously added new content based on player feedback.

By the time Minecraft officially launched in 2011, it had already amassed a substantial fan base. At this moment, Persson decided to hand over creative control to Jens Bergensten, a fellow game developer at Mojang. This allowed Persson to step back and let fresh ideas and perspectives drive the game's continued evolution. Under Bergensten's leadership, Minecraft continued to develop new elements that enabled players to create even more complex and imaginative structures.

The success of Minecraft didn't go unnoticed by the broader tech industry. In 2014, as rumors of a potential Mojang initial public offering (IPO) swirled, Microsoft stepped in and acquired the studio for a staggering $2.5 billion. This acquisition marked a new chapter for Mojang and Minecraft, as it provided the resources and support needed to expand the Minecraft universe even further.

With Microsoft at the helm, Mojang Studios launched several new versions of Minecraft, including a free Chinese edition in collaboration with NetEase in 2016 and an education edition aimed at schools and educators the same year. These new versions broadened the game's appeal and introduced it to new audiences around the world. Minecraft Education Edition, in particular, demonstrated the game's potential as a learning tool, helping students develop skills in areas like math, science, and coding through interactive and engaging gameplay.

By 2022, Minecraft had become a cultural phenomenon. It generated $365 million in revenue that year, and 90 million people played the game at least once a month. The game's sales had surpassed 300 million copies across all formats, making it the best-selling video game in history.

Recommended Reads

Launch Your Book with a Bang by Abbie Emmons.

- Abbie Emmons shares her perfected book launch marketing strategy, which helped her achieve #1 New Release status on Amazon during the preorder stage. The training covers finding your readers, nurturing a loyal fanbase, creating promo posts, connecting with influencers, and more.

Starting a Business QuickStart Guide: The Simplified Beginner's Guide to Launching a Successful Small Business by Ken Colwell, PhD MBA.

- This comprehensive guide covers essential aspects of starting a business, including creating a business plan, marketing strategies, securing funding, and more. It's a valuable resource for new entrepreneurs.

Chapter 8:

Mastering the Money

Oftentimes, people spend money like the way they drive. Whether you have a car or not, here's a scenario you've surely experienced. Say you're in heavy traffic. You're stuck, frustrated, and you notice the lane next to you seems to be moving faster. Naturally, you're tempted to switch lanes, but as soon as you do, that lane comes to a halt, while your original lane starts moving. Ugh!

Yet, the impatience described above (justifiable at times) often translates to many people's spending habits. Constantly changing your financial plans on a whim or based on current trends often leads to more frustration and less progress. This is a big reason why people without financial management skills tend to lose their money or grow at a painfully slow pace.

Financial management helps you make sure you have the resources you need for unexpected events, take advantage of opportunities when they arise, and avoid the stress that comes with financial uncertainty. It also teaches you the difference between needs and wants. It's tempting to spend money on things that bring immediate pleasure, like the latest gadget or a night out. But you should always put your long-term goals over short-term desires. This doesn't mean you can't enjoy life. Never that. You just have to find a balance that ensures your future is secure while still relishing the present.

Leveraging Data and Technology

Modern accounting software that can automatically track your income, expenses, and profit/loss, are becoming increasingly ubiquitous. The insights you get from using modern tech to decipher the financial needs of your business can help you avoid potential cash flow issues.

You can be seen as a wise and reliable leader if you work using data and technology. Similarly, by using financial planning software, you can create detailed financial projections and scenarios, allowing you to plan for different outcomes.

Selecting Simple Financial Management Tools

Before you start exploring the various financial management tools available, you need to know what you need. You need a clear understanding of the kind of business you are running and the level of complexity of your financial transactions. Knowing those details, do you think you need a tool that can handle payroll, invoicing, and inventory, or will you be better served by something simpler that tracks income and expenses?

If your business involves international transactions, for instance, you might need a tool that supports multiple currencies. On the other hand, if your primary focus is on managing expenses and income, a simpler tool will suffice. Learn your needs, and you'll be able to narrow down your options and avoid paying for features you don't need.

Here are some popular financial management tools and apps that are suitable for teen entrepreneurs:

- 22Seven: This local financial app and website is known for its personal finance monitoring capabilities, but it's also useful for business purposes. You can monitor all your financial activities by linking 22Seven to your business banking account.

- Zoho Books: Zoho Books is an excellent online accounting software for small and medium-sized enterprises. It not only manages your finances but also automates many of your business's workflows.

- Xero: Xero has a range of tools specifically designed for small business owners. One of its standout features is its ability to link seamlessly with accountants and bookkeepers, saving them the hassle of downloading data and sending numerous emails. Xero is user-friendly and can give you an eagle's eye over your financial health.

- QuickBooks: QuickBooks is a great bookkeeping app for entrepreneurs. It provides local sales and support services, and importantly, allows transactions in multiple currencies. QuickBooks caters to various business needs, from payroll to tax filing. It's an excellent choice for teen entrepreneurs looking to manage their finances efficiently. As far as financial management software goes, this is heavy duty compared to the lighter alternatives mentioned in this list.

Most financial management tools come with free or budget versions. These versions often include essential features that are more than sufficient for a startup. Zoho Books and QuickBooks discussed above both have free trials or basic plans with the fundamental tools needed to get started. This allows you to test the software without committing financially.

Making the Right Choice

As we've seen, there is no shortage of financial management tools that entrepreneurs can rely on. But you can't use them all (nor should you, *really*). You need to select the ones that help you stay ahead of financial challenges. Here are some tips to help you make the right choice:

- Evaluate your needs: As mentioned earlier, start by assessing your business's specific financial management needs. List out the features that are critical for your operations.

- Research and compare: Take the time to research different tools. Compare their features, pricing, and user reviews. Look for tools that offer free trials so you can test them out before making a decision.

- Seek recommendations: Talk to other entrepreneurs or mentors about the tools they use.

- Scalability: Choose a tool that can grow with your business. As your business expands, so will the complexity of your financial management needs. Ensure that the tool you choose can accommodate this growth.

- Ease of use: Go for tools that are user-friendly and have good customer support. This will make the learning curve less steep and ensure you can get help when needed.

Step-by-Step Exercises to Create a Budget

Creating a budget might sound boring, but it's super important for your business. It helps you manage your money, plan for future expenses, and make sure your business is successful in the long run. Here's a simple guide to help you set up a budget for your custom sneaker business.

Identifying Costs

First, you need to figure out all the possible expenses. There are two types of costs you need to think about:

A. Initial costs

These are the expenses you'll have before your business officially starts. For a custom sneaker business, they might include:

- materials for prototyping: $100 for fabric, leather, and adhesive.

- design software: $50 for a basic subscription to design software.

- marketing materials: $100 for flyers, social media ads, and promotional items.

- business registration: $50 for registering your business name and any necessary licenses.

B. Ongoing costs

These are the regular expenses you'll need to cover once your business is up and running:

- materials for production: $200 per month for sneaker materials.

- marketing and advertising: $100 per month for social media ads and promotions.

- shipping costs: $50 per month to send your products to customers.

- utilities: $50 per month for internet and phone bills.

- miscellaneous: $50 per month for unexpected expenses.

Estimating Revenues

Next, you need to estimate how much money you'll make each month. This can be tricky, but it's an important part of planning your finances.

A. Research your market.

To make accurate revenue estimates, you need to know your market. Look at competitors and analyze their pricing and sales volumes. This can give you a sense of what you might realistically achieve.

B. Define your revenue streams.

Identify all your potential sources of income. Some common revenue streams for a custom sneaker business might include:

- Product sales: Estimate selling 20 pairs of custom sneakers per month at $50 each, totaling $1,000 in monthly revenue.

- Service fees: If you provide custom design services, estimate 5 clients per month at $20 each, totaling $100 in monthly revenue.

C. Make conservative projections.

When estimating your revenues, it's better to be conservative. Start with a baseline scenario based on minimal sales, and then create more optimistic scenarios. This will help you prepare for different outcomes and reduce the risk of overestimating your income.

Planning for Savings

You should also plan for savings. Set aside a portion of what you make for future investments and to cover unexpected expenses.

A. Emergency fund

Keep an emergency fund to take care of unexpected costs. Aim to save enough to keep your business running for about three to six months.

B. Future investments

Plan for future growth by saving for investments in new technology, additional staff, or expanded marketing efforts. Regularly set aside money for these purposes to ensure you're prepared to scale your business when the time is right.

C. Contingency planning

Always have a contingency plan. This means being prepared for the possibility that your revenues might not grow as quickly as expected or that you might face unforeseen costs. Having a financial cushion can make the difference between weathering a tough period and going out of business.

Practical Exercise for Creating Your Startup Budget

Let's put theory into practice with a simple exercise to help you create your startup budget.

Step 1: List Your Initial Costs

Take a piece of paper or open a spreadsheet and create a detailed list of all the initial costs you can think of. Be thorough and consider every possible expense. Here's a quick example to get you started:

- materials for prototyping: $100

- design software: $50

- marketing materials: $100

- business registration: $50

- total initial costs: $300

Step 2: Identify Your Ongoing Costs

Next, list your monthly ongoing costs. Use a similar level of detail as you did for the initial costs. Example:

- materials for production: $200

- marketing and advertising: $100

- shipping costs: $50

- utilities: $50

- miscellaneous: $50

- total monthly ongoing costs: $450

Step 3: Estimate Your Monthly Revenues

Based on your market research and business plan, create a conservative estimate of your monthly revenues. Example:

- product sales: $1,000

- service fees: $100

- total monthly revenues: $1,100

Step 4: Plan for Savings

Decide how much you will set aside each month for savings. Example:

- emergency fund: $100

- future investments: $50

- total monthly savings: $150

Step 5: Create Your Budget Document

Combine all this information into a comprehensive budget document. It might look something like this:

Initial costs:

- materials for prototyping: $100

- design software: $50

- marketing materials: $100

- business registration: $50

- total initial costs: $300

Monthly ongoing costs:

- materials for production: $200

- marketing and advertising: $100

- shipping costs: $50

- utilities: $50

- miscellaneous: $50
- total monthly ongoing costs: $450

Monthly revenues:

- product sales: $1,000
- service fees: $100
- total monthly revenues: $1,100

Monthly savings:

- emergency Fund: $100
- future Investments: $50
- total monthly savings: $150

Tips and Strategies for Making Good Spending Decisions

It goes without saying that no business would have a chance at thriving or even surviving if the entrepreneur tends to make poor choices. As a leader, you should always pay attention to where your money is coming from, where it's going, and how to manage it effectively to ensure your business's growth and stability. Admittedly, this sounds daunting, but with the right strategies and tools, you too will master it.

Try the strategies below to improve the savviness of your spending decisions.

Understanding Your Financial Position

This is the first step in improving the quality of your choices. When you know your financial position, this means you have a clear picture of your business's financial health at all times. You want to be the kind of business leader who monitors their cash inflows (the money coming into your business) and outflows (the money going out). You'll be able to see patterns in your spending and identify areas where you might be able to cut costs or make adjustments by keeping track of your general cash flow.

You also want to make like a seer and estimate your future income and expenses based on past performance and future plans. This act is called a financial projection. It can help you anticipate potential cash flow issues and plan for them in advance.

Importance of Saving for Future Growth and Unexpected Expenses

People, especially those leading a business, save a portion of what is earned to afford themselves a financial cushion for tough times and provide stability for future growth. Here are some common reasons why saving is important:

- Investing in future growth: Saving money also provides you with the capital you need to invest in your business. Whether it's purchasing new equipment, expanding your marketing efforts, or hiring additional staff, having cash on hand can help you take advantage of growth opportunities and take your business to the next level.

- Elevating your reputation: Developing good saving and investment habits can also make a positive impact on your stakeholders and investors. They will see that you are frugal and want to make every penny go a long way. This can do wonders for your reputation and increase your chances of attracting investors, who'll be more confident in your ability to manage their money effectively.

Practical Tips for Saving Money

To help you save money and build that financial cushion we talked about, employ some practical tips:

- Automate your savings: Create a system where money is sent to your savings account automatically. This can help you build your savings over time without having to think about it.

- Cut unnecessary expenses: Regularly review your expenses and look for areas where you can cut costs.

How to Calculate Profit, Understand Loss, and Determine the Break-Even Point

You need to understand these concepts to be able to assess the financial health of your business and make the right decisions as a leader. Let's start with the first one.

Calculating Profit

Profit is the financial reward for a business when the money it makes exceeds what it spends. To calculate the profit gained by any business, follow these steps:

1. Determine the cost price of the products sold: This is the total expense incurred in producing or purchasing the products that are sold.

2. Calculate the total selling price of the products sold: This is the total revenue generated from selling the products.

3. Subtract the cost price from the selling price to get the profit amount: Profit = Total Selling Price - Total Cost Price

Example:

So you run a small business selling custom-sneakers. Every pair of sneakers costs you $20 to make (cost price), and you sell each one for $100 (selling price).

So, the profit for each sneaker sold would be:

Profit = Selling Price - Cost Price

Profit = $100 - $20

Profit = $80

If you sold 10 pairs of sneakers, your total profit would be:

Total Profit = 10 X $80

Total Profit = $800

Understanding Loss

A loss in finance refers to the negative difference between total costs and total revenues, where costs exceed revenues. In simpler terms, a business incurs a loss when it doesn't bring in enough money to cover its expenses.

Example:

Let's consider the same sneaker business, but this time, due to a mistake, you priced the sneakers at $10 each, while the cost to make each one remains $20.

So, the loss for each sneaker sold would be:

Loss = Cost Price - Selling Price

Loss = $20 - $10

Loss = $10

If you sold 10 sneakers at this price, your total loss would be:

Total Loss = 10 X $10

Total Loss = $100

Determining the Break-Even Point

The break-even point is used to figure out the minimum number of sales you need to make to cover all your costs. It's the point where your total costs and total revenue are roughly the same value. Here's how you calculate it:

Break-Even Quantity = Fixed Costs / (Sales Price per Unit - Variable Cost per Unit)

Fixed Costs: Costs that don't change, no matter how much you sell (e.g., basic supplies, website fees).

Sales Price per Unit: How much you sell each item for.

Variable Cost per Unit: How much it costs to make each item.

Example:

Imagine you started a business selling custom sneakers. Here are your figures:

Cost price per sneaker: $50

Selling price per sneaker: $150

Fixed costs per month: $1,000

Step 1: Calculate the Profit for Each Sneaker Sold

Profit per sneaker = Selling Price - Cost Price

Profit per sneaker = $150 - $50

Profit per sneaker = $100

Step 2: Calculate the Total Profit if You Sell 200 Sneakers in a Month

Total Profit = 200 x $100

Total Profit = $20,000

Subtract the fixed costs to find the net profit:

Net Profit = $20,000 - $1,000

Net Profit = $19,000

Step 3: Calculate the Break-Even Point

Using the break-even formula:

Break-Even Quantity = $1,000 / ($150 - $50)

Break-Even Quantity = $1,000 / $100

Break-Even Quantity = 10 sneakers

This means you need to sell 10 sneakers each month to cover your costs. Selling more than 10 sneakers will generate a profit, while selling fewer will result in a loss.

Understanding Taxes

Right alongside the thrill of running your own enterprise comes the not-so-enjoyable but necessary task of understanding how taxes work and how to deal with them. Let's go over the basics you need to know.

Income Tax

Income tax is a tax on the money you earn. If you're self-employed and earn $400 or more, you are required to file a tax return, regardless of your age. This might sound surprising, but it's important to remember that the IRS (Internal Revenue Service) views all income earners equally when it comes to taxes. The amount of tax you owe will depend on your total earnings for the year (Self-employed individuals, n.d.).

The income earned by many teenage entrepreneurs might not be substantial enough to owe a lot of tax. This is because you can apply the standard deduction, which often reduces your taxable income to zero, meaning you might not owe any income tax at all. However, you still have to file your tax return to report your earnings.

Self-Employment Tax

In addition to income tax, self-employed individuals are also responsible for self-employment tax. This tax covers Social Security and Medicare, which are usually withheld from an employee's paycheck by their employer. As a self-employed individual, you need to pay these taxes yourself. About 15.3% of your net income (profit) should be remitted as self-employment tax.

For example, if your business makes a profit of $1,000, you will owe approximately $153 in self-employment tax.

Sales Tax

Sales tax is another important consideration, especially if you are selling goods or services. This tax is collected whenever goods or services are sold, and the rules can vary depending on your state. In some states, you may need to collect sales tax from your customers and then remit it to the state government.

The frequency of these payments can vary. Some states require annual payments, while others may ask for quarterly or even monthly payments, depending on the amount of sales you make. It's important to check your state's specific requirements to ensure you're in compliance.

Financial Obligations

One of the keys to successfully managing your taxes as a teen entrepreneur is keeping meticulous records of your business activities. This includes recording all sales and receipts, as well as any business-related expenses. Money spent on growing your business, such as purchasing supplies, advertising, or even a portion of your home used for business purposes, can often be claimed as deductible expenses on your tax return. These deductions reduce your taxable income, potentially lowering your tax bill.

Since taxes are not automatically withheld from your earnings as they would be in a traditional job, it's up to you to save a portion of your income to cover your tax bill. A good rule of thumb is to save about 25-30% of your profits for taxes, which should cover both income and self-employment taxes.

Keep in mind that the information in this section shouldn't be seen as a substitute for official tax advice. It's just some general info and best practices. Make sure you talk to a CPA once your business gets going to make sure you're setting aside enough for taxes.

Success Stories

Mikaila Ulmer

Mikaila is an extraordinary entrepreneur who grew a simple lemonade stand into a thriving business known as "Me & The Bees Lemonade." Her journey from a young girl with a homemade recipe to a successful businesswoman is nothing short of remarkable.

This story begins with Mikaila's great-grandmother's 1940s lemonade recipe, which includes flaxseed and honey from local beekeepers. This recipe, the cornerstone of what would become her flourishing business, not only gave her brand a unique flavor but also a purpose—to help save the bees. Her parents, D'Andra and Theo Ulmer, both equipped with business degrees, nurtured Mikaila's budding entrepreneurial spirit from a young age.

At just four years old, Mikaila was encouraged by her parents to participate in a children's business competition. While brainstorming ideas, she found herself on the wrong side of a bee's stinger, all in one week. Initially fearful of bees, Mikaila turned this fear into fascination, learning about their critical role in our ecosystem. This newfound knowledge, combined with her great-grandmother's recipe, sparked the idea of adding honey to her lemonade, promoting both a tasty drink and a vital cause.

Mikaila started selling her honeyed lemonade in front of her house in 2009. Her refreshing lemonade soon became the talk of the town, attracting the attention of a local pizza shop. As demand grew, Mikaila's parents helped her scale up the production, and "Me & The Bees Lemonade" began its expansion into various local stores.

Although she wanted to make a profit, Mikaila was more committed to donating 10% of her profits to organizations dedicated to saving the bees. Many people warmed up to her brand because of this socially responsible approach.

In 2015, Mikaila appeared on the television show Shark Tank with her father. Standing confidently in front of seasoned investors, Mikaila pitched her lemonade business. Her impressive presentation and the unique value proposition of her product caught the attention of Daymond John, who invested $60,000 to support her growing business. This investment provided the necessary resources to expand the production and distribution of her lemonades.

The journey from running a small lemonade stand to having a nationally recognized brand was not without its challenges. But Mikaila's determination and her family's support helped her achieve one win after the other. In 2017, her perseverance paid off when a consortium of football players invested $800,000 into her company. This substantial investment allowed "Me & The Bees Lemonade" to increase its production and expand its market reach.

Soon, Mikaila's lemonade was in about 500 shops in America. Her business continued to grow, and by February 2020, "Me & The

Bees" could be found in more than 1,500 stores across the country. Her product line also expanded to include lip balms made from beeswax.

Currently, Mikaila is enrolled as a student at Emory University, balancing her academic pursuits with her business responsibilities. In August 2020, she published her book, "Bee Fearless, Dream Like a Kid," through Penguin Random House. The book chronicles her adventures as a young entrepreneur and offers valuable insights into building a purpose-driven brand.

Mikaila Ulmer's story is a testament to the power of passion, perseverance, and purpose. Here are some nuggets that you should take from her experience:

- Tell your unique story: Mikaila's success is deeply rooted in her personal story and family tradition. Embrace what makes you unique and use it to differentiate your brand.

- Combine passion with purpose: Mikaila's passion for lemonade and her commitment to saving bees created a powerful brand message. Find a cause to champion and make it a core part of your business model.

- Find support and mentorship: Mikaila's parents were instrumental to her success. They gave her the guidance and support she needed to win. To get the same results, don't hesitate to seek help from family, mentors, or business networks.

- Stay resilient in the face of challenges: The path to success is famously rocky. Mikaila faced numerous challenges but remained resilient. This is an attitude worth emulating. You want to look for the lessons in your setbacks, learn from them, and keep moving forward (People who inspire, 2018).

Donald Dougher

Meet Donald Dougher, a young American entrepreneur born in 2006. Donald, often known by his online moniker Donlad, grew from an ordinary teenager into a well-known social media star through sheer creativity, hard work, and business savvy.

Donald launched his YouTube channel in August 2019, a decision that would change his life forever. From the beginning, his content stood out. He created a variety of videos that included lifestyle content, pranks, and collaborations with other popular YouTubers, and this attracted a wide audience. His subscriber count climbed rapidly and today, his channel boasts over 550,000 subscribers.

One of Donald's most memorable videos is one where he gives a Rolls-Royce to FaZe Rug, another famous YouTuber. In this video, his fans got to witness his generosity flair for creating engaging and entertaining content. Donald's collaborations with well-known YouTube stars like Tanner Fox, Piper Rockelle, and the Funk Bros further boosted his popularity. His fans, affectionately known as #Ladiators, are always thirsty for the latest video from Donlad.

But Donald's success is not confined to YouTube. In 2020, he ventured into the world of business by starting his own clothing brand, FAT CAT. His entrepreneurial spirit shone through in how he managed and marketed this new brand, proving that he had a knack for business as well as entertainment.

Donald's ability to juggle multiple ventures at such a young age is remarkable. His parents, Yvonne and Don, and his older sister, Sophia, often appear in his videos, providing his viewers with a glimpse into his supportive family life. Their involvement highlights the importance of a strong support system in achieving success.

One of the most impressive aspects of Donald's story is his financial acumen. Despite his young age, he has demonstrated a sophisticated understanding of money management. His net worth is estimated to be around $1 million, a figure that many adults aspire to but few achieve. Donald earns his money through various streams, including ad revenue from YouTube, brand partnerships, and his clothing brand.

Donald's approach to money is both practical and visionary. He understands the importance of saving and investing, and he is always looking for new opportunities to grow his wealth.

There are a few things we can learn from Donald Dougher's story:

- Diverse income streams: Donald's success is partly due to his ability to generate income from multiple sources.

- Smart investments: Investing in his clothing brand was a smart move that has paid off significantly. It shows the importance of investing in ventures that you are passionate about and that match your personal brand.

- Hard work and dedication: Donald's rise to fame was not overnight. It took consistent effort, creativity, and dedication to build his YouTube channel and his brand.

- Family support: Having a supportive family has been crucial to Donald's success. Their involvement in his ventures has provided both emotional support and practical assistance.

- Financial literacy: Donald's ability to manage and grow his wealth at such a young age highlights the importance of financial literacy. Understanding how to manage money, invest wisely, and diversify income is non-negotiable for long-term financial success (Stefan, 2023).

Recommended Reads

MONEY Master the Game: 7 Simple Steps to Financial Freedom by Tony Robbins.

- Tony Robbins provides a seven-step blueprint for achieving financial freedom. Based on interviews with legendary investors, the book covers the topics of control over financial decisions, savings, and investing.

Rich Dad Poor Dad by Robert T. Kiyosaki.

- Kiyosaki shares lessons from his "rich dad" and "poor dad." The book emphasizes financial education, assets, and passive income to achieve wealth.

Chapter 9:

Next Big Steps After Success

After an initial burst of success, many businesses face the hurdle of maintaining momentum without losing their core values or overextending their resources. We had talked about the need to always keep the ball rolling. But it's equally important to discuss the how. In this chapter, we'll explore various strategies that young entrepreneurs like yourself can employ to scale their businesses sustainably. You'll discover how to leverage creative and cost-effective growth methods, like using customer feedback as a valuable tool for improvement. And that's just the tip of the iceberg. Let's get to it already!

Customer Feedback Collection and Analysis

Getting feedback can be done in several ways. Surveys, for instance, are a tried-and-true method for gathering data from your customers. They allow you to ask specific questions about your product, service, and overall experience. A well-done survey can help you discover trends and preferences that aren't immediately obvious.

Social media, too, is a major player in collecting feedback. But we've already gone through the process of leveraging this opportunity in the previous chapters of this book. So, we'll move smoothly on to direct communication.

Sometimes, nothing beats a simple phone call or a chat on social media. These options are super easy and totally free, making them perfect for getting personal with your customers. Phone calls and social media interactions can give you deep insights that surveys might miss. What your customers say is important, but how they say it—their tone, their expressions, and what they emphasize—matters even more. If you need to dig deeper, surveys can be a great extra tool, but starting with phone calls and social media is the way to go.

When you're reaching out to customers, here are some questions you should ask to get valuable feedback:

- "What do you love most about our product/service?" This helps you understand your strengths from the customer's perspective.

- "Is there anything you find frustrating or difficult?" Identifying pain points can guide you on what to improve.

- "How did you first hear about us?" This can provide insights into which of your marketing efforts are working.

- "What other products or services would you like to see from us?" This can reveal opportunities for expanding your offerings.

Start with a friendly introduction and explain why you're reaching out. Keep the tone casual and conversational, not like a formal survey. Listen actively and show appreciation for their feedback. If you're using social media, create posts that encourage your audience to interact with you. Ask open-ended questions and engage with the responses you get.

Making Your Customers Happy

A happy customer not only returns but also tells others about their great experience. That's right. You can make your customers so satisfied that they basically become unpaid salespeople for your company. In fact, this brand evangelism is the most definitive measure of a business that's actually solving a problem. So how do you convince your customers to go from skepticism to loyalty to advertising your brand for free?

The first piece in the puzzle is something we've already touched on (although it demands reiteration): customer service. As much as possible, your interactions with your customers should be positive. Your brand should always be approachable, attentive, and prompt in its response to issues. Even when dealing with complaints or outright insults, be calm and respectful.

You can pull your customers closer by personalizing your interactions with them. Use their names, remember their preferences, and note important details from previous conversations. This small gesture will almost certainly make them feel special. It shows that you view them as individuals, not just sales figures. It helps to see your customers as sort of external team members. They're not outside your company but, if everything goes right, active participants in your success. So, keep them in the loop by providing them with timely updates about their orders or any changes concerning your services.

Another effective strategy is to provide exclusive content or perks for your most loyal customers. This could be early access to new products, special discounts, or behind-the-scenes looks at your business. Again, such rewards will make them feel appreciated and part of an inner circle.

Envisioning the Future: Long-Term Planning and Adaptability

As we wrap up our discussion on scaling a business sustainably, keep in mind that your initial success is only the beginning. What comes next will demand a solid foundation and an awareness of the ever-changing tides of the entrepreneurial sea in which you swim.

So far in this chapter, our position essentially emphasized the importance of balancing creativity with financial prudence. You most likely won't overstretch your resources if you make smart and educated choices. Businesses that grow too quickly without proper planning often find themselves overwhelmed by increasing demands and operational complexities. This can lead to financial strain, loss of quality in products and services, and ultimately, business failure. On a wider scale, irresponsible growth can impact your community and the environment negatively, eroding customer trust and damaging your brand's reputation.

You really shouldn't hurry the process.

Your journey to growing in a sustainable way needn't be a race. See it as nurturing a plant instead. It needs the right balance of water, sunlight, and care to grow strong and healthy. With patience, diligence, and a willingness to learn and adapt, your business will flourish.

Case Studies of Happy Customers

Apple

Apple's success is not just due to its innovative products and marketing strategies, but also its incredibly loyal customer base. This loyalty is so strong that it manifests in interesting ways, like customers camping outside Apple Stores for days, eagerly awaiting the release of new products.

One notable instance of this loyalty was observed in Australia, where a customer was seen camping outside an Apple Store even before any official announcement of new devices. Despite Apple's attempts to correct this trend, the tradition of camping outside stores has continued. Angela Ahrendts, Apple's retail chief, emphasized the convenience of online shopping in an internal memo to store staff. She encouraged employees to inform customers about the ease of ordering online, stating, "Get in line online. The days of waiting in line and crossing fingers for a product are over for our customers. The Apple Store app and our online store make it much easier to purchase Apple Watch and the new MacBook. Customers will know exactly when and where their product arrives" (Campbell, 2015). This initiative by Angela was meant to reduce the physical lines and make the purchasing process smoother and more predictable for customers.

Yet, the persistence of this camping tradition shows that for many, the excitement of being among the first to own a new Apple product and the camaraderie of the experience is irreplaceable. This dedication is now a cultural phenomenon that sets Apple apart from other tech companies.

Let's see one case study of a dedicated Apple customer who embodies this phenomenon. Meet Sam, a 25-year-old tech enthusiast from Sydney, Australia. Sam is an avid Apple fan who has been following the company since his teenage years. For Sam, Apple's product launches are no different from a holiday.

In 2023, news started circulating about a potential new iPhone release. Although Apple hadn't made any official announcements, the buzz was enough to get Sam excited. He decided to camp outside the Apple Store in Sydney to make sure he would be among the first to get his hands on the new device. Sam arrived at the store three days before the anticipated announcement, equipped with a camping chair, a sleeping bag, and a portable charger. During his three-day campout, Sam met other enthusiasts, exchanged stories about past product launches, and shared tips on how to make the most out of Apple devices. This camaraderie and shared excitement made the wait enjoyable and memorable.

Trader Joe's

For many customers, Trader Joe's is a cherished part of their lives. One such testament to this passion is the podcast "Inside Trader Joe's," which, although not officially affiliated with the company, captures the spirit and enthusiasm of its fans.

"Inside Trader Joe's" is a popular podcast series that discusses various facets of the Trader Joe's experience. It's important to note that this podcast is created by fans of the store, not the company itself. This distinction shows us the genuine appreciation and enthusiasm that the creators have for Trader Joe's. This is a true labor of love. The podcast gives listeners a glimpse into the inner workings of Trader Joe's.

The podcast also discusses diverse issues that keep the content fresh and engaging.

One episode might analyze the fascinating process behind setting prices at Trader Joe's. Unlike many grocery stores that follow industry trends, Trader Joe's employs a unique pricing strategy that often involves cutting out middlemen to offer lower prices to customers. This behind-the-scenes look helps listeners appreciate the effort and thought that goes into making their favorite products affordable.

Another episode might shed light on the latest products perfect for air frying—a popular cooking trend. Whether it's crispy cauliflower gnocchi or perfectly seasoned chicken tenders, these episodes provide practical tips and inspiration for incorporating Trader Joe's products into everyday meals. Such episodes are a hit among listeners who love experimenting with new recipes and cooking methods.

Trader Joe's enjoys a loyal customer base, but like any business, it has its share of mixed reviews. Many customers praise the friendly and helpful staff, noting that their shopping experience is always pleasant. The unique and high-quality products also receive high marks, with customers often raving about their favorite finds, from the famous "Everything but the Bagel" seasoning to the decadent chocolate lava cakes. But some customers have expressed concerns about the quality of certain items, particularly meat products. There have been instances where the meat did not meet expectations, leading to disappointment

Despite these mixed reviews, Trader Joe's remains a popular choice for many shoppers. The store's commitment to providing unique products at affordable prices, coupled with a welcoming atmosphere, continues to attract a dedicated following. It's this community of loyal customers that fuels the success of initiatives like the "Inside Trader Joe's" podcast.

In-N-Out Burger

In the subculture of fast food, there exists a niche that thrives on whispers and insider knowledge. This culture revolves around the secret menu of In-N-Out Burger. Among the enthusiasts who have immersed themselves in this hidden culinary world, one name stands out: Sam Vonderheide. Known for his adventurous spirit and love for unique culinary experiences, Sam has turned his exploration of In-N-Out's secret menu into a celebrated venture that's captured the hearts of many.

In-N-Out Burger is an iconic institution on the West Coast, famous for its simple and delicious menu. But beyond the publicly displayed items lies a hush hush menu that has been passed down through word of mouth and online forums. This secret menu features a variety of burger modifications, extras, drinks, and treats that cater to the adventurous palate.

Popular Secret Menu Items

- Animal Style (Burger): This fan-favorite includes pickles, an overload of In-N-Out's famous sauce, grilled onions, and mustard fried onto each patty.

- Flying Dutchman: A minimalist's dream, the Flying Dutchman consists solely of two beef patties and two slices of cheese, sans buns. It's the purest form of beef and cheese for those who crave simplicity.

- Toasty Buns: For an added crunch, this modification involves frying the buns, giving them a delightful crispness that enhances every bite.

- Grilled Cheese: Perfect for vegetarians, this sandwich replaces the meat with melted cheese, combined with the usual fresh lettuce, tomato, and special sauce.

- Protein Style: For those seeking a low-carb option, the Protein Style burger substitutes the buns with crisp lettuce, wrapping all the flavors in a refreshing, crunchy package.

- Well-Done Fries: These fries are cooked a bit longer to achieve a crispy texture, making them a perfect side for any burger on the menu.

So how does Sam Vonderheide fit into all this?

Sam and his friends have made it their mission to explore and document their experiences with In-N-Out Burger's secret menu. This mission has taken them to various In-N-Out locations, where they've tried different secret menu items and shared their findings online.

Through social media platforms and video-sharing websites like YouTube, Sam and his friends have chronicled their adventures, giving reviews and tips to fellow fast-food enthusiasts. Their content is engaging, informative, and often humorous.

Despite the mixed reviews often found in the fast-food industry, In-N-Out Burger has managed to maintain a strong and loyal customer base. While some customers have faced issues with the quality of the meat or the company's handling of service animals, many others have praised the friendly staff, consistent quality, and the excitement of the secret menu.

Many customers, like Sam, have had overwhelmingly positive experiences at In-N-Out Burger. They appreciate the clean and welcoming atmosphere, the fresh ingredients, and the ability to customize their orders.

Recommended Reads

The 7 Habits of Highly Effective People by Stephen R. Covey.

- This classic book emphasizes personal effectiveness and provides practical principles for achieving success in both personal and professional life.

Drive: The Surprising Truth About What Motivates Us by Daniel H. Pink.

- Pink explores motivation, autonomy, and purpose, offering insights on how to stay driven and fulfilled in your career.

Chapter 10:

Turning Failure to Success

Too often, we perceive failure as a definitive sign we've reached our limits. Young entrepreneurs who pour their time and energy into launching, say, a product only to face poor sales might react with frustration or self-doubt. Perhaps they think of famous business icons—like Bill Gates or Oprah Winfrey—and assume these figures never faced setbacks. However, the reality is quite different; most successful people faced numerous failures before finding their way. The problem isn't failing itself; it's how we interpret and react to those failures that define our future actions.

In this chapter, you'll discover practical strategies to manage emotional reactions to setbacks and learn methods for extracting valuable lessons from each misstep. We will explore resilience-building practices and share real-world examples of entrepreneurs who turned their failures into catalysts for success.

Changing the Mindset Around Failure

You've probably never thought of this way, but failure is not the opposite of success; it's a part of it. When you think about starting a new business, you might feel a crippling fear of getting it all wrong. And this is a common reaction of many entrepreneurs. Society often portrays successful entrepreneurs as individuals who magically got everything right from the start. However, most successful people will tell you that they're students of failure. They, like anyone faced with the same decisions, made many wrong turns and detours on their journey to success. But they managed to tame their instincts to give up.

Recall Thomas Edison's famous quote, "I have not failed. I've just found 10,000 ways that won't work." Each of his "failures" brought him closer to an invention that changed the world. What if he had given up after his first try? That's something to think about.

When you view failure as a chance to learn, you become more willing to take risks and step out of your comfort zone. You begin to see each attempt as a chance to gather valuable information that will guide you toward eventual success. You start thinking like an investigator, dissecting each failure for clues and using what you learn to refine your strategies. When a good scientist, for instance, conducts an experiment, and it doesn't yield the expected result, they don't see it as a wasted effort. Instead, they analyze what went wrong, adjust their hypotheses, and try again and again. This iterative process is where true progress happens. So, why should entrepreneurship be any different?

Rather than throwing in the towel because your plans fell flat, take a step back and ask yourself: What did I learn from this? Perhaps the feedback you get from this kind of introspection will show you a feature your product is missing, or maybe it'll reveal a new market segment you hadn't considered.

This attitude will take resilience to pull off. And, interestingly, the more resilience you practice, the more resilient you'll be. It's very much like building muscle. We'll talk about resilience later in this chapter.

When reflecting on a failure, it's beneficial to break it down into components. Ask yourself: What was within my control? What was beyond it? Doing so will help you identify actionable items to improve upon while letting go of factors you couldn't influence. This analytical approach is often successful at making the process less scary.

If you want to think about failure differently, accept the fact that you'll never outgrow the need to learn. Tuning your mindset toward continuous learning rather than immediate success will give you so much staying power. Lifelong learning keeps you adaptable and open-minded. If a specific business strategy didn't pan out, investigate alternative methods and educate yourself on best practices in that area. While doing this, be self-compassionate. Beating yourself up over failures will only drain your energy and dampen your motivation. Instead, be kind to yourself. Recognize the courage it took to try, and give yourself credit for every lesson learned.

Managing Emotional Reactions to Failure

When you think about failure, do you automatically feel a wave of disappointment, panic, self-doubt, or worry? These emotions are common and very human, especially when things don't go as planned.

Disappointment often comes from unmet expectations. You want to be a business owner, so you've certainly imagined yourself winning at this game. You've thought of the accolades, profits, and happiness that your success would bring. If the reality doesn't match up, disappointment can set in. It's similar to how you'd feel missing out on a much-anticipated concert because tickets sold out; you're left with a void where excitement once was.

You might start questioning why things went wrong despite all your hard work. Frustration can make you want to give up entirely because it's exhausting to continuously face obstacles. And then self-doubt creeps in quietly and starts eroding your confidence. You begin to question your abilities, your worth, and whether you were cut out for this entrepreneurial path in the first place.

These reactions are normal, but they don't have to define your response. This is not an encouragement to suppress these feelings, but to manage them constructively. Here's what you can do to turn these emotional responses into powerful learning moments:

- Take a deep breath and acknowledge your emotions.

- Reflect on the situation by asking yourself critical questions like, what exactly went wrong? Was it something within your control or external factors?

- Talk it out with someone you trust.

Once you've processed your emotions constructively, the learning can start. Here are some actionable strategies to help you learn from failure:

- Keep a journal or a log of what happened, what you tried, and what the outcomes were. This way, you have concrete data to analyze later.

- Conduct a post-mortem analysis. Ask questions in this direction: Did the marketing strategy fall short, or was it the product itself that didn't meet customers' needs?

- Seek feedback from mentors, peers, or even customers.

Remember, these strategies shouldn't serve as a one-time fix. They are best utilized as ongoing processes. The more you engage in reflective practices, the better you'll become at navigating failure.

Developing Mental Resilience

One effective approach to build mental resilience is positive thinking. By this, you are encouraged to focus on solutions rather than problems. Constantly remind yourself, even in the thick of it, that what went wrong isn't nearly as important as what you can do better. As such, you can become resilient not through wide-eyed optimism that things will always be good, but that failure presents you with an opportunity to mine wisdom.

Try these ideas to become more resilient:

- Start each day by listing three things you're grateful for.

- Whenever a negative thought pops up, counter it with two positive thoughts. For instance, if you think, "I messed up that presentation," immediately remind yourself of two previous successes you've had.

You can also help your resilience by always being present. This means you should be focused on the moment, rather than getting lost in worries about the future or regrets about the past. When you practice mindfulness, you'll find yourself better equipped to handle stress because you can observe your thoughts and feelings without getting overwhelmed by them.

Try incorporating mindfulness into your daily routine:

- Dedicate a few minutes of your morning to quietly focus on your breathing. Pay attention to each inhale and exhale. If your mind starts to do its thing and move to other thoughts, take air into your lungs, breathe out, and try to concentrate on the life-giving act of breathing again.

- Throughout the day, take short breaks to check in with yourself. Notice how you're feeling and what you're thinking. Even a brief moment of awareness can help reset your mind and reduce stress.

Stress Management Techniques

Starting a business is inherently stressful, which means you'll have to find healthy ways to cope with that stress. This might involve physical activities, hobbies, or relaxation techniques that help you recharge.

Consider these approaches:

- Engage in regular exercise, whether it's a sport you love, yoga, or even just a brisk walk.

- Develop a hobby that allows you to unwind and escape from the pressures of work. This could be anything you love, really.

- When you feel stressed, take a moment to breathe deeply. Inhale slowly through your nose, hold the breath for a few seconds, and then exhale slowly through your mouth.

It also helps if you have a growth mindset. This means knowing that it's up to you to develop your abilities and intelligence. For this reason, people with a growth mindset are often more relaxed and resilient.

Do these to foster a growth mindset:

- When you encounter a difficult situation, remind yourself that this is an opportunity to develop new skills.

- Begin to think of effort, painful though it is, as the only path to gaining mastery. Understand that achieving anything worthwhile requires hard work and persistence.

- Instead of taking feedback personally, use it as constructive input to improve your performance.

Facing Challenges and Finding Solutions

Starting a business as a young entrepreneur can feel like walking through a minefield. For a while, it might seem like the game has been rigged against you in particular. The crippling combo of financial constraints, lack of experience, and frequent criticism can make even the fiercest visionary question the merit of their venture. But every successful entrepreneur has navigated these challenges, and so can you. One by one, let's tackle these common hurdles (which really should be seen as rites of passage).

Running out of Money

The lack of easy and quick access to funds is often the first stumbling block. Money, a unique concept in nature, is one of the biggest stressors that you'll face as a business owner. Thankfully, there are practical ways to mitigate this issue:

- Begin by drawing up a budget that outlines your necessary expenses. This will help you understand how your money should be spent and saved.

- Look for funding options such as small business grants, crowdfunding, or even pitching your idea to investors who may see potential in your vision.

- Even though it's the 21st century, you can still barter services with others. If you have skills or resources that another entrepreneur needs, and vice versa, negotiate with them.

Little or No Experience

It's a fact of human psychology that our level of confidence is often tied to our level of experience. It's easy to feel overwhelmed when you're starting out and don't have a track record to lean on. The more you experience about the world, the less you might feel like you need your parents. This principle holds true in business, since you'll become more confident about your choices as you gain experience. With more experience is also at play in the world of business.

How do you gain this experience? Well, you're on the right track so far. You should gain knowledge by reading books like this one, and apply what you learn. You can also try these:

- Consider internships or part-time jobs in industries related to your business idea.

- Online courses and workshops offer flexible ways to gain knowledge and skills. Sites like Coursera, Udemy, and Khan Academy host a wealth of information on various subjects.

- Seek mentors who have traversed this path before.

Recommended Reads

The Other 'F' Word: How Smart Leaders, Teams, and Entrepreneurs Put Failure to Work by John Danner and Mark Coopersmith.

- Danner and Coopersmith provide actionable insights for harnessing failure as a powerful tool for innovation and growth.

Failing Forward: Turning Mistakes into Stepping Stones for Success" by John C. Maxwell.

- Maxwell dissects the anatomy of mistakes and shows how they can become steppingstones to success. He offers practical strategies to transform failure from a regret into a resource, emphasizing personal and professional growth.

Chapter 11:

The Balancing Act

Many aspiring young entrepreneurs struggle with feeling overwhelmed by their responsibilities. You may feel the same way, too, when you start your business, and it's entirely understandable. Even as a young person, you might have to juggle homework, extracurricular activities, and personal interests before even considering business tasks. The truth is that the adventure you're about to undertake won't be easy.

While you should avoid being lazy, it's also important that you don't fall into the trap of constant busyness. In business, motion doesn't always mean progress. For instance, spending hours writing emails or making minor website tweaks might feel like a productive way to spend your time, but these tasks might be detracting from more impactful efforts like product development or marketing strategies. You need clear priorities to make sure you attend to the most important tasks first.

This chapter will guide you through a variety of effective strategies to help you manage your time and set priorities that matter most to your business aspirations. You'll learn how to establish clear, actionable goals and develop routines that'll boost your productivity without compromising your mental health.

Time Management Tips

As we stated earlier, you may often feel overwhelmed by the myriad tasks and responsibilities vying for your attention as a leader. But not to worry. There are proven strategies that can help you organize your time efficiently.

- Have a goal: Take some time to identify what you want to achieve, both in the short-term and long-term. Would you like to launch your product by the end of the year? Do you want to secure a certain number of customers within six months? You need a sense of direction and purpose to lead your business toward success, and having precise, measurable goals will provide you with this virtue.

- Reduce your goals: No, this doesn't mean that you should dream small. Instead, you should break down your goals into smaller, actionable steps. Create a to-do list every day, and write each one in order of their relevance to your ultimate goal. Pro tip: you can categorize your business tasks into what must be done now, what can wait, and what can be delegated.

- Develop a routine: Consistency is the perfect pairing for productivity. They go so well together, you often can't have one without the other. This doesn't mean you need to rigidly stick to a schedule that leaves no room for flexibility. Instead, find a rhythm that balances work and rest, maintaining your energy levels throughout the day.

- Keep track of how you spend your time: Use tools like planners, apps, or even simple spreadsheets to log your activities and see where your time goes. This can reveal surprising patterns and help you identify areas where adjustments could free up more time for important tasks.

Maintaining Motivation

Your motivation needs to come from a place that's deeply personal to you. Maybe it's the desire to achieve financial independence, create something innovative, or make a positive impact in your community. Whatever it is, this core motivation will be your anchor during hard times. When you're clear about why you're doing what you're doing, it becomes much easier to stay committed, even when external circumstances are less than ideal.

No journey is ever smooth. There will always be bumps along the road. But as we've explained in this book, each hurdle you encounter can teach you something valuable about your business, your market, and yourself. Instead of getting discouraged, ask yourself: What went wrong? How can I prevent this from happening again? What can I learn from this experience?

To stay motivated, you need to be able to manage your stress levels effectively. High-stress levels can quickly sap your enthusiasm and productivity. So, take a few minutes each day to meditate, practice deep breathing, or engage in a relaxing activity can help you stay grounded and centered. A calm mind is more resilient and better equipped to tackle challenges head-on.

If that doesn't do the job, you can also try visualization. Imagining your success vividly can do wonders for the level of your motivation. Take a moment each day to visualize achieving your goals. Try to see every detail—the sights, sounds, and feelings associated with your success—with your mind's eye. This practice can create a powerful mental image that'll keep you moving forward, even when the going gets tough. You can balance this process by also journaling what you see during the visualization exercise and the actual progress you're making toward the realization of your dream.

Another aspect worth mentioning is your environment. Where you are can sap your motivation and courage or make you feel powerful. Sometimes, physical surroundings can influence our mood and productivity. So, you want to create a workspace that's organized, inspiring, and free from distractions. It is simple, everything around you should contribute to your focus and creativity.

In all, remember to take out time for rest and recuperation. The chapter is about balance, and you should always strive to achieve an equilibrium with any of your strategies. It's tempting to want to push yourself non-stop as the competitive and passionate entrepreneur you probably are. But remember that burnout is real and can be detrimental to your progress. Balancing work with adequate rest ensures that you're operating at your best. So take regular breaks and try to always have a good night's sleep, as these are investments in your long-term sustainability.

Key Takeaways

- Although time is a finite resource, you can absolutely control how you use it. One effective method is setting specific and achievable goals for each day.

- Maintaining motivation can be tricky, especially when facing long-term projects or the inevitable setbacks. Here, understanding your "why" can make all the difference. Keeping your purpose front and center can fuel your motivation during tough times. Surround yourself with reminders of why you started—whether it's vision boards, motivational quotes, or regular meetings with a mentor who inspires you.

- Identify what's urgent versus what's important. These aren't always the same thing. Many times, we get caught up in tasks that seem urgent but do little to move us toward our bigger goals.

- Life can be unpredictable, and sometimes plans will change. You should be able to switch things up and take a different direction if you have to.

- Self-care might sound cliché, but know that you can't pour from an empty cup. You should take care of your physical and mental well-being if you want to stay productive. Simple things like getting enough sleep, eating nutritious foods, and making time for relaxation can keep you energized and focused.

- Setbacks are inevitable aspects of running a business. But if you can learn how to bounce back effectively, they won't bother you as much. It's important to look at setbacks not as failures but as learning opportunities. Each one brings with it valuable lessons that can help you improve and grow. Reflect on what went wrong, but also on what went right, and use this insight to adjust your course moving forward.

- Consider practicing resilience by changing your perspective on challenges. Instead of seeing them as roadblocks, accept that they're merely puzzles waiting to be solved. By doing so, you'll find that you're curious and determined, instead of feeling stressed and frustrated.

Recommended Reads

Getting Things Done: The Art of Stress-Free Productivity by David Allen.

- Allen's classic guide presents organizational systems and best practices for managing tasks and workflow. The book emphasizes tackling tasks as they come to prevent overwhelm and reduce stress. It introduces the GTD system, helping readers organize workflows effectively.

Deep Work: Rules for Focused Success in a Distracted World by Cal Newport.

- This book provides a masterclass in tuning out distractions and hyperfocusing. It aims to make you a Jedi at concentrating. The second half of the book includes tips for working more efficiently, such as blocking out social media and achieving peak "deep work."

Conclusion

You maintained the momentum and made it to the end. You truly are made of the right stuff. This book challenged your ability to evolve, and you stepped up.

Now, the real test begins!

From the moment you close this book and lift your head, you're presented with two choices: Will you apply what you've learned, or will you let your dream die unhatched? Optimistically, you'll choose the first path and become a hero!

In the intro, you were promised five lessons to help you win on your hero's adventure:

- how to get a business idea

- how to test the idea

- how to make a plan

- how to secure the funds you need to start

- how to scale up and maintain your growth

You might agree that this book not only delivered on its promise but went the extra mile to make what should be difficult ideas quite accessible. You've also been furnished with stories of young people like you who've made their dream work. It's time to dig deep.

Be prepared for the challenges on your path to greatness, but keep in mind that those obstacles are only powerful relative to the strength of your resolve. If you commit yourself to never-ending learning and are determined to stay the course, you'll certainly undergo a metamorphosis and become a champion.

So, go out there, do the thing, and become the achiever you know you can be!

Glossary

Authenticity: Being real and true.

Boundaries: The edges of something.

Challenges: Hard tasks.

Dedication: Sticking with something important.

Developing: Making something better.

Discoveries: Finding new things.

Entrepreneur: A person who starts their own business.

Excitement: Feeling very happy and eager. Failures: Times when things don't work out.

Invention: Making something new.

Investors: People who give money to help a project grow.

Innovators: People who create new ideas or things.

Leaders: People who guide others.

Magnetic: Very attractive or interesting.

Marketing: Promoting and selling things.

Obstacles: Things that make it hard to move forward.

Origin: The start of something.

Partners: People who work together.

Passion: A strong love or excitement for something.

Planning: Making detailed plans.

Pursuit: Chasing after something.

Radioactivity: Energy from certain atoms.

Reenergize: Getting your energy back.

Science: Learning about nature and the world.

Self-awareness: Knowing yourself well.

Setbacks: Problems that slow you down.

Strategy: A plan to reach a goal.

Suffering: Going through pain.

Visionaries: People who think about the future in a new way.

References

Hostaway (n.d.). *Airbnb founders: Brian Chesky, Nathan Blecharcyzk, and Joe Gebbia.* https://www.hostaway.com/blog/airbnb-founders/

Byer, J. (2024). *Unique Value Proposition: What it is, why it's important, how to create a UVP, and 10 examples.* Crowdspring. https://www.crowdspring.com/blog/unique-value-proposition/

Campbell, M. (2015, April 7). Angela Ahrendts tells retail employees to push customers online for Apple Watch, 12" MacBook launches. AI. https://appleinsider.com/articles/15/04/07/angela-ahrendts-tells-retail-employees-to-push-customers-online-for-apple-watch-12-macbook-launches

Dutra, J. (2022). *What did Socrates, Plato, and Aristotle think about wisdom?* The University of Chicago. https://wisdomcenter.uchicago.edu/news/wisdom-news/what-did-socrates-plato-and-aristotle-think-about-wisdom

Moore, K. (2014). *Inspiring stories of mentors who made a difference for small business owners.* Grasshopper. https://grasshopper.com/blog/inspiring-stories-of-mentors-who-made-a-difference-for-small-business-owners/

People who inspire: Mikaila Ulmer, the unstoppable 13-year-old social entrepreneur. (2018). Shondaland. https://www.shondaland.com/inspire/a20688383/microsoft-mikaila-ulmer-me-and-the-bees-lemonade/

Porter, K. (2024). *Creating a budget that works for you.* Rocket Money. https://www.rocketmoney.com/learn/personal-finance/the-definitive-guide-to-creating-a-budget-that-works

Prouty, A. (2022). *'There's always a good somewhere': First Stage brings the inspiring true story of Alex Scott to life.* Spectrum News 1. https://spectrumnews1.com/wi/milwaukee/news/2022/05/06/the-amazing-lemonade-girl-marcus-center-first-stage-alex-scott-alexs-lemonade-foundation-play-true-story-childhood-cancer

Quezada, V. (2017). *How these teenage sisters turned a $25 science experiment into a successful company — all before they graduated high school.* Money. https://money.com/teenage-sisters-turned-a-25-science-experiment-into-a-successful-company-all-before-they-graduated-high-school/

Scheps, L. (2021). *Teen sisters run a $20 million business selling bath bombs we all need right now.* Inside Edition. https://www.insideedition.com/teen-sisters-run-a-20-million-business-selling-bath-bombs-we-all-need-right-now-63871

Self-employed individuals tax center. (n.d.). IRS. https://www.irs.gov/businesses/small-businesses-self-employed/self-employed-individuals-tax-center

Sharma, A. (n.d.). *Shravan and Sanjay Kumarana.* The CEO Magazine. https://www.theceo.in/leaders/shravan-and-sanjay-kumaran

Stefan, C. B. (2023). *Donald Dougher Net Worth | Parents.* Famous People. https://famouspeopletoday.com/donald-dougher/

Walters, M. (2023). *The evolution of The Last Of Us's Bella Ramsey.* The List.

https://www.thelist.com/1189634/the-evolution-of-the-last-of-uss-bella-ramsey/

Williams, G. (2011). *Hart Main, ManCans: 13-year-old entrepreneur invents candles for men.* Huffpost. https://www.huffpost.com/entry/hart-main-mancans-13-year-old-entrepreneur_n_909300

www.ingramcontent.com/pod-product-compliance
Lightning Source LLC
Chambersburg PA
CBHW022040190326
41520CB00008B/656